Taking Care of Mom & Dad

A Beginner's Guide to Caring for Your Parents

Taking Care of Mom & Dad:
A Beginner's Guide to Caring for Your Parents

Copyright © 2016

Authored by:

Dominique Alvarez (Visiting Angels of Chino & Diamond Bar, California)
William Bruck (Visiting Angels of Monroe, Michigan)
Page Cole (Visiting Angels of Tulsa & Bartlesville, Oklahoma)
Debra Desrosiers (Visiting Angels of Auburn, New Hampshire)
David Forman (Visiting Angels of Southern Delaware)
Paul Gach (Visiting Angels of Charlotte, North Carolina)
Debbie Harrison (Visiting Angels of Grand Junction, Colorado)
Valerie Hentzschel (Visiting Angels of Prescott, Arizona)
Patty Laychock (Visiting Angels of Atlantic County, New Jersey)
Gail Lohman (Visiting Angels of Cameron Park, California)
Margaret Maczulski (Visiting Angels of Libertyville, Illinois)
Bob Melcher (Visiting Angels of Fairfield, Connecticut)
David Milby (Visiting Angels of Central Georgia)
Tina Moore (Visiting Angels of Belleville, Illinois)
Eddie Morris (Visiting Angels of Ponca City, Oklahoma)
Susie Murray (Visiting Angels of Cleveland, Georgia)
Deborah Waldecker (Visiting Angels of Sun City Center, Florida)

This title is also available as an eBook from Amazon.com

Table of Contents

Foreword

YOU ARE NOT ALONE.

Let that sink in for a minute. At any given moment, there are THOUSANDS of adults just like you who are struggling with the same challenges, stresses and even heartaches of living as family caregivers for their aging parents.

You are not alone in these struggles.

You are not alone in trying to navigate through these difficult issues either. This book is the compilation of years of both personal and professional experience in helping family caregivers successfully deal with the worries and work of parenting one's own parents.

This book is not intended to be a technical journal, nor a step by step manual for avoiding the problems of living as a member of the Sandwich Generation. Rather, it is simply a group of educated and skilled senior care professionals having a friendly conversation with you, offering their encouragement, wisdom and a little hope as you walk this challenging road. Although the individuals who compiled this book are all owners of a Visiting Angels franchise, this book is not a work written or published by the national franchise.

If you or your family have questions about home care for a loved one, you can find a local Visiting Angels office by going to www.visitingangels.com, or by calling toll free 800-365-4189 for more information.

Disclaimer: The views expressed here are solely those of the authors in their private capacity and do not in any way represent the views of the Living Assistance Services, or any other entity. This book is intended to be a tool of encouragement and guidance, not a technical or legal resource.

Dedication

There are so many individuals and groups who have helped make this project come to fruition. The authors who sacrificed their time in the midst of busy schedules running their own home care agencies are to be commended. Their work in the trenches has brought an invaluable tool together to be used as a guide for the many families facing the challenges of caring for a loved one!

The corporate staff at Visiting Angels have been so supportive and helpful in this process as well. Their dedication and expertise in supporting hundreds of Visiting Angels franchises across the country have insured that families across the United States and around the world receive the highest level of care. Their dedication to that worthy task is only further highlighted by their support of this project.

This dedication would be incomplete without a specific "shout out" to Larry Meigs and Jeffery Johnson, the founders of Visiting Angels. Their vision for setting the standard in quality home care for everyone else to follow continues to be realized year after year. Their encouragement, hard work and belief in franchisees has made Visiting Angels Americas Choice in Home Care!

Finally, this work is dedicated to family members who continue to care for their loved ones in need. In spite of hectic work schedules, busy personal lives and stresses that come with everyday living, the sacrifices of these caregivers cannot go unnoticed. They deserve our respect, our applause and our honor as they pour out of their own lives into the lives of their aging loved ones. We hope and pray this resource is helpful to them as they continue in their caregiving journey.

Preface- "How Can I Tell If My Parents Need Help?"

So the big question of questions is this… "How can I tell if Mom and Dad need help?" I wish there was one or more easy answers to that question, but life is just not that simple! In the chapters to come, the various authors will offer you their insights regarding warning signs or symptoms that might tip you off that your parents are needing your assistance. Regardless of which topic you are addressing in the coming chapters, consider these suggestions as you look for signs that might indicate you need to step in and help your parents.

Watch

Often the best thing you can do is simply quietly observe what is happening with your parents in their daily activities of living. Take note of their motor skills, their level of clear communication, and even their cognitive abilities. Is their ability to drive safely diminishing? Do they have trouble explaining to you what they need? Do they seem to be more and more forgetful?

Ask

You can't be afraid to have honest and direct discussions with one or both of your parents. It may be that one of your parents is more needy than the other parent, and you can have a more honest discussion transparent dialogue with them about what kind of assistance they need. If both parents are genuinely in need, then as difficult as that discussion might be, be direct in asking if they could use help managing their finances, keeping up with the house, driving or other activities.

Listen

You may be able to glean an abundance of knowledge about your parents condition by listening to them talk to you, your siblings, the grandchildren or others. Sometimes they will "tattle" on themselves about areas they are struggling with or needs they could use assistance in meeting.

Taking Care of Mom & Dad

*A Beginner's Guide to
Caring for Your Parents*

PART ONE- LEARNING AND UNDERSTANDING YOUR PARENTS CARE NEEDS

Chapter 1- Hiring an Agency v. Private Hire

Susie Murray

When it comes to Caregiving, does it matter who is providing the care?

One of the biggest concerns with almost anything in our lives is cost. This is especially true when it comes to the cost of caring for loved ones in the home. There are many variables for which there are no sure answers. For instance:

- "My parents only need 8 hours a week now, but will they need 20 hours in 6 months? Will they eventually need 24-hour care? How much money do we actually need?"

When you take these unknown factors into consideration, it is easy to panic and feel the need to start cutting costs. This results in one of the big questions of home care: Which is best- hiring a private contractor versus hiring a home care agency?

Obviously, you can hire a private caregiver for less money, since there is no agency as a "middle man". Depending on the state in which you live, you can hire a private caregiver for anywhere from $10-$15 per hour. Again, depending on your state, an agency may charge anywhere from $16-$30 per hour. For the sake of this discussion, let's settle on an average cost of a private caregiver charge of $12 per hour and agency cost of $20 per hour.

As an owner of an agency, this is one of the big arguments I face when dealing with potential client inquiries. Potential clients say, "Why should I pay you $8 more per hour than I would Mary? She seems just as qualified as one of your caregivers as you describe them. She is a CNA, has 10 years of experience and has a flexible schedule. Tell me why I should pay so much more to hire you?"

There are many positives to hiring an agency. In a nutshell, at a time in life when you need help the most, a home care agency will do the worrying for you. Whether we are talking about care for your spouse or your parents, a sibling or a grandparent, the last thing in the world that you need at this moment in time is another job and the stress that comes with it. After all, isn't that why you are reaching out for help in the first place? Let's break it down into a few basic segments:

Scheduling, Coverage, and Caregivers – What a Headache!

Ask any agency owner what the biggest challenge of our profession is; nearly everyone will tell you the greatest challenges are employees and scheduling. We love our caregiving staff! At the same time, they can drive us crazy. From top to bottom, the whole health care industry is one that is prone to high turnover; for many reasons this is particularly true among home care workers. Comparing the number of caregivers hired each year to the number of resignations/terminations for the year reveals an industry standard of 60%, per the 2015 Private Duty Benchmarking Study by HomeCare Pulse.

Home care workers tend to seek the relationships they can forge with their individual client or couples, because they can't do that in a nursing home or hospital. They also tend to seek the flexible schedule that they can find in this niche because they can't do that in a facility either. Do you think a facility cares that they have three kids of various ages, or that their husband works the swing shift, so they need to work the graveyard shift? The facility is going to dictate to the caregiver what her work schedule will be. The home care worker may be a retiree who is not up to the rigors of facility work and restrained by the requirements of a social security income, but still need to make some extra money. She may have school age kids that she is staying home with, and only able to work 15-20 hours per week. She may only be able to work evenings or weekends due to another job. Home care agencies tend to be much more flexible in scheduling and working with their staff, making it a more desirable work field for many caregivers.

Home care workers know that he or she is giving up higher pay and benefits often earned in a hospital or nursing home, but in return earns the rewards of flexibility and actual care for clients that she earns in home care. As a result, for the scheduler and owner, there's a fine line of pampering and firmness involved. I was a business management major, and I remember a professor who made a profound impact on me. His philosophy was that as a manager, one can't treat each employee the same way. With some caregivers the home care agency needs to be stern, while others may need to be treated with kid gloves in a unique situation. Some staff will need a shoulder to cry on from time to time, while others might be embarrassed by sentiment. I've learned these lessons in life as well, but it has been poignant in remembering one particular class in my dealings with caregivers; some act tough and rough around the edges. I have found that by the nature of what they do, they are frequently fragile individuals whom have been shaped by often tragic circumstances. These caregivers need time and attention to be their best. Caregivers also need clear and fair expectations in their role in the home. One of the most important factors in making your decision about whether to hire a private caregiver or an agency centers around these staff management issues. Each caregiver is an individual, but agency leaders have learned how to navigate these confusing and difficult personnel issues.

Additionally, as the condition of your loved one deteriorates, are you prepared to provide on-going training? Do you have a Registered Nurse on staff to be able to provide hands on training for that caregiver on the best way to handle a bed-bound patient, demonstrate catheter care, or how to figure out the sling on the Hoyer lift? Also, do you have the ability to conduct background checks and do drug screenings? Do you know the laws and have policies in place concerning privacy laws and the caregiver's rights in regards to background checks and drug screenings? What about tuberculosis screening and the law about offering hepatitis B inoculation? You can bet that your licensed agency does. You may encounter legal problems due to injuries, communication or tax issues that you were unaware of when you chose to hire privately. These questions are not intended to make you feel inadequate to care for your loved one, but rather to show you the broad scope of issues that are involved in that process.

Do you have the time for this staff development if you are dealing with high levels of care? The great thing about hiring an agency is, we are doing this for you. This is our dilemma. If your loved one needs daily care, then you need at least two caregivers. Daily care of eight hours, at least three.

Twenty-four-hour care, seven days per week? Four to six caregivers, due to the current labor laws. Without an agency, you've just given yourself another full time job as a recruiter and scheduler!

Consider another important issue; what happens when your private caregiver calls in sick? Most likely, you as the family caregiver will have to fill the gap, or no one shows up at all. When you've hired a home care agency that just became the responsibility of the agency. I've committed to you that I will have someone there to take care of your loved one. That's why I have a large and qualified staff. I do not like surprises, so I have rules in place to make sure that we keep these instances to a minimum, but everyone and their children get sick, so when an absence is inevitable, I have multiple caregivers to fill the gap. It will never be something that you have to worry about.

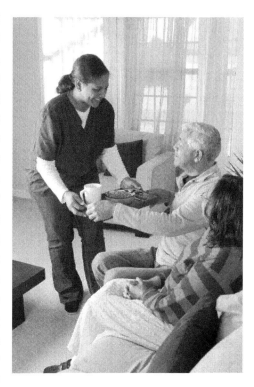

Wage and Hour Laws

Unless you are a business owner yourself or in human resources, you've probably never considered "wage and hour" laws. This is where the government starts getting into your business. If you plan to issue a 1099 to your private duty employee to write off health care expenses, then you should pay attention.

Until recently, the caregiving industry operated under the "caregiver exemption" policy, which meant that in many states the home care workers could work more than forty hours per week without being paid overtime or paid minimum wage. (Not being paid minimum wage would apply to "live in" jobs, when the caregiver would be staying for days on the premises and sleep time would be factored into the equation.) This has been a contentious piece of legislation since it was last decided upon in the 1970s. When the Obama administration came into office in 2009, it had the stated goal of the abolition of the Companionship Exemption as a key priority of its domestic agenda. While this case is still waiting to be reviewed by the Supreme Court (2016), early indications are that the Supreme Court will rule in favor of the forty-hour week plus overtime scenario. So, your private caregiver may be willing to work over forty hours per week for you without charging you overtime because that has always been the case. Knowing the previous federal case rulings and the indications of the Supreme Court, agencies are already prepared and following the future case law. What will your private caregiver do?

Here is a likely scenario: your private caregiver is dedicated to you. Once this is the law of the land, attorney bill boards will start to pop up and commercials may start playing about "money you are rightfully owed as a caregiver". You could quickly find yourself involved in a very expensive wage and hour suit that you have no chance of winning. Regardless of how loyal your caregiver is, money nearly always speaks louder than words.

I have really oversimplified things here. To get the entire picture and specifics regarding this issue, go to the Department of Labor's final rule, most frequently asked questions on domestic home care workers, found here: http://www.dol.gov/whd/homecare/faq.htm. This is critical for your long term financial security regarding homecare- if your caregiver does anything other than sit and talk to your loved one for more than eight hours out of a forty-hour work week, he/she qualifies for minimum wage and overtime, regardless of what type of other outstanding living arrangements you may have agreed upon. In the event you lose a lawsuit, you would be responsible for back wages, penalties, interest and legal costs. On the other hand, you could just hire a home care agency!

Worker's Compensation Insurance

It is highly unlikely that your private caregiver is carrying Workers Compensation insurance on themselves. I've never talked to a private caregiver that does carry their own Workers Compensation policy. Workers Compensation is the insurance that covers a caregiver if she were to be injured in your home during the course of caring for your loved one, or even slip on the proverbial banana peel. As agency owners, this is usually our highest percentage cost of doing business, other than labor itself.

Many people think that their homeowner's insurance will always cover this sort of thing. That is absolutely not true. Even if it does cover a claim, your homeowner insurance rates will likely skyrocket in the event of a claim like this. If your caregiver were to be injured on the job and you are not carrying Workers Compensation insurance, you will get sued. In addition, you need to check with your state to see what laws and penalties may apply to individual employers and domestic workers. Please do not think that signing a simple "hold harmless" clause will be sufficient. This is how families lose their homes and their personal worth.

Unfortunately, even agencies aren't completely "covered" by worker's compensation insurance. It is more of a financial tool than complete insurance. Worker's Compensation insurance is based on estimated number of caregiver hours to be worked in the upcoming calendar year. At the end of the year, owners receive a bill or a refund for the difference, so it is important to plan for the unexpected. An employer's premium will also be adjusted for any claims presented during the calendar year. In very basic terms, I see a worker's compensation policy existing to cover any *catastrophic* and *immediate* loss; there will be reckoning at the end of the year, and I know that I need to be prepared for it. If my agency incurs any losses, I need to be ready with a check to cover that total amount at the end of the year. An owner I know wrote a $32,000 check at the end of 2015 for one claim. Basically, if you are an employer, the system stinks. Last year, my small agency had a payroll of $320,000. I think of my worker's compensation premium as a $22,000 employee that I never see. That number is sure to jump in the near future, as the premium amount tends to rise pretty much dollar for dollar with claims amounts.

There are, of course, very complicated insurance formulas involved in this process. You can use a search engine for "Workers Compensation calculations" and come up with all sorts of confusing and conflicting information if you choose to do so. I'm deliberately eliminating it from this discussion because it is more complicated than this chapter warrants.
The bottom line is this: if you are hiring a private caregiver, you are taking the world of Workers Compensation into your own hands. Honestly, it is a headache most families do not need, and a risk they do not want to take. If your caregiver gets injured, has medical bills, and is no longer able to work, money will once again trump loyalty, and the caregiver is actually owed compensation and care. If the caregiver is dishonest with one of those hard-to-disprove soft tissue injuries, you are probably going to pay out the nose for that as well.

Tax Reporting
Is your private caregiver an employee for whom you are responsible for reporting and paying payroll taxes, or an independent contractor? This can be tricky and can depend on the state in which you live. You'll have to consult an accountant and possibly a tax attorney to make the wisest decision and it could be dependent on the status of your loved one's estate. There are lots of possible variables here. At the very least, you are going to require a W-9 and issue a 1099.

Although home care is considered non-medical in nature, for tax purposes, home care is considered a medical expense. Thus, you want to capture this for your and/or your loved one's tax return. The only way to take advantage of this tax break is to also issue a 1099 to your private caregiver. A 1099 eliminates being able to take advantage of the tax credit without also paying the legally required payroll taxes. Some private caregivers prefer to be paid "under the table" in an attempt to avoid their own tax burden. This is a discussion you'll want to have upfront with any caregiver you hire. You need to represent your best interests here and make sure that the caregiver is in agreement and amicable.

Be sure to check the requirements in your state for the withholdings for domestic workers. You do not want to get caught on the wrong side of the Department of Labor. Fines can add up quickly and most laws in this arena are state specific.

Advantages of Hiring a Private Caregiver?

The greatest advantage of hiring a private caregiver is that when you first hear the hourly cost (without thinking of the risks, worries and work that go along with it) it sounds great because it is a few dollars per hour cheaper. When you multiply that hourly savings out over time, it looks to be substantially cheaper. If you are very fortunate and your tenure of caring for your loved one goes completely without incident of any kind, it may work out that way for you. That may be a risk you are willing to take. If so, you are one of the people that I wish all of the best, and ask that you keep my number handy and remind that I'm available in case of emergencies.

As agency owners, we truly do wish the best for those that choose not to go with our services. We want, but honestly couldn't handle, all of the business inquiries that come our way. Good help is the hardest thing in the world to find. It is because of this that we know that we will be hearing from some of you again, unfortunately, after you've hit some rough times.

When a family member tells me that she has decided to hire her own caregiver(s) instead of choosing my agency, she inevitably tells me it is either to save money, to help someone out who needs a job, or because the person came highly recommended. In cases where a loved one only needs a few hours of care per week, it may work out well for a while.

I normally get a call back in 20% of these cases within one year, asking for services because things didn't work out well. However, if it is a case of a higher need client (eight plus hours per day or more), I remind the family member that my agency is available for emergency fill-ins when her caregiver calls out sick or is unavailable. In 40% of cases that happens within the first month. In 24-hour care cases, private caregivers are simply unable to sustain the level of care required for any length of time beyond a few days, and I would estimate that in 70% of those cases, my agency is providing fill-in caregivers or taking over care within two weeks.

These private caregivers mean well, but unless they don't have a spouse, no children, no pets, and no need to sleep, it is simply not possible to provide that level of care for a sustained period of time. As an agency owner, I'm always willing to step in and share time with the private caregiver, because it is making sure that the client is receiving the care that they deserve. However, private caregivers tend to be very territorial!

Bottom line, when you and your family are trying to determine whether or not hiring an agency or a private caregiver is best for your unique circumstance, do not let anyone tell you what's best for you. But make your decision with all of the facts, challenges and risks laid out before you, and choose what's best for your family. This means not only comparing hourly rates, but considering potential financial risk, stress, tax and insurance liabilities and so much more! Good luck, and if you still have questions, call a Visiting Angels to find out more information. You can find out the closest office to you by calling 1-800-365-4189, or visit the website at www.visitingangels.com for more information!

Chapter 2- Honey Your Parents Are Moving In
Debbie Harrison

The statement "Honey, your parents are moving in" is not quite as frightening as "Honey, I shrunk the kids!", but it is a close second! My husband's grandparents all lived well into their 90s, and it appeared that his parents would as well. Tom's parents were the ones who cared for each set of grandparents as they declined, so in 2005 Tom and I started talking to his parents about their plans should the good Lord (always good to play the God card) grant them the lifespan their parents had enjoyed.

We listed off some scenarios:
1. God would grant their wish to die peacefully in their sleep. (Envision St. Peter guiding them to heaven as cherubs play beautiful music)
2. Tom and I would quit working, move to small town Colorado near them to be at their beckoned call night and day. (Envision both my husbands' and my tombstone, with Mom and Dad sobbing at the graveside)
3. They would move into a Nursing Home. (Not a visual anyone wants)
4. They would come to live with us. (Envision the Walton's)

Mom and Dad are sensible people, so after much discussion we all agree on option four! Walton's Mountain, here we come! We started planning a custom home which would be built to accommodate the four of us under one roof (one very big roof). We shared every step of the process with Mom and Dad, mailing blue prints, land photos, color swatches and progress reports along with photos. It was a group effort and all was going surprisingly smooth (hmmmm?). We added features like zero thresholds, two master suites, wider doors, grab bars in the bathroom and an extra-large garage. Dad could tinker, mom could wander freely with her walker, and everyone would have their own space. We were on the road to success! We had it all! We were very proud of our new home and ourselves.

We flew Mom and Dad up for the housewarming party! They loved everything we had done. They praised our efforts and sat proudly in the living room as the guests asked if they liked their new home. "Oh yes, I can't believe our kids would do all this for us" was heard on several occasions. "We are so blessed to have such caring children" was another statement. We pictured Norman Rockwell looking down from heaven wishing he could paint our portrait...Success!

Tom and I were beaming with pride; remember that's what goes before the fall! We were confident that we had the future figured out. Until…the day before mom and dad were scheduled to return to Colorado and they said there was just one little problem; they were not going to move to Alaska! Did I leave that part out? Yes, our beautiful new home was in Wasilla, Alaska (if that sounds familiar, we could see Sarah Palin's mayoral office from our kitchen window). It was not like this was a big secret. Tom and I had lived in Alaska the majority of our adult lives. When asked why they didn't say something sooner they said, "Well, honey you were so excited we didn't want to hurt your feelings". WHAT?!! This never happened on The Waltons TV show!

We put Mom and Dad on the plane, tucked our tails between our legs and started thinking about "Plan B". Okay, the truth is, we cussed and fumed, kicked the dirt and said "they can just go to the nursing home and see how they like that!" We carried on for a few days (maybe weeks) but somewhere around January, when the snow was four feet deep, the temperature dropped below zero, and we only saw the sun for five hours a day, we realized they might have a point.

Many of us have friends or co-workers who receive that phone call from a hospital (typically in the middle of the night) saying one of their parents has had a medical emergency. This often happens without warning due to a health event or a fall and it never seems to happen at a good time. Tom and I had watched as many of our friends in Alaska were forced to deal with these emergencies from thousands of miles away. We decided we would rather be proactive than reactive, so we sat down to develop "Plan B" which would have to include our exit from the frozen north land.

Given that we were still in our fifties and needed to continue to work, the first step was to decide what we were going to do to make a living in Colorado. Of course, Mom and Dad lived in a small community (with little opportunity for employment) 50 miles outside of Grand Junction (the big city). I had been heavily involved in the Real Estate industry, and Tom had managed the coffee shops we owned. It was 2007 and the real estate market was declining (understatement?). We figured the economic decline of the mid 2000's would have an adverse effect on the viability of making a living selling $4 cups of coffee (unless you name it after a celestial body and a four-legged animal). What to do? Decisions, decisions...we have often relied on prayer for guidance, so we started there.

Soon Tom and I realized we had always been drawn to the elderly. We enjoyed their company and stories. We had spent a lot of time with the seniors in our church and were sympathetic to their life changes as they aged and declined in health. We thought about lines of work that would bring us happiness, a paycheck, and would benefit Mom and Dad as well. We eventually decided (or all that praying opened our ears) that if we were going to change our lives for octogenarians why not figure out how to make a living in the field with the added bonus of getting the inside track to find the best services for Mom and Dad. Okay, we have a "Plan B". Nothing to it. Sell everything we own (including a brand new house). Get rid of all our adult kids' cherished belongings that they couldn't part with but somehow couldn't get out of our crawl space either. Find a good home for the dog (mom's allergic to the dog). Sell the coffee shops and the extra car. And do all this without telling my employer that we were leaving (I gave 6 weeks' notice but the selling started 6 months earlier). Sure; that'll work! And let's figure out how to break into a brand new industry in a brand new town!? Piece of cake!

As luck would have it, (remember the prayer part), I heard a commercial for Visiting Angels Living Assistance on my way to work. After a little research we decided to pursue a franchise. The first step was to attend a short seminar presented in, of all places, Denver, Colorado. We flew to Colorado, attended the seminar, and our future was set. Fast forward another year and we had pulled it off! Colorado here we come! It was going to be a new adventure, a new beginning. After all, your fifties are the new thirties. Why not reinvent yourselves? We loaded up the F-350 crew cab with the few belongings we kept and headed south. For those of you that do not immediately remember the cost of fuel in June of 2008, let me remind you. They were the highest prices in history. When you factored in the exchange rate, an imperial liter to a gallon, we paid $6.43 per gallon for diesel fuel through Canada. For those of you that do not immediately think about the size of Canada let me tell you, it is BIG!! The upside of the high cost of fuel was we had the Al-Can highway to ourselves.

We have a plan, we have cut our old ties, and we are off to a new start! We will get to Colorado, Mom and Dad will welcome us with open arms, and we will be like the Walton family on television! One big happy family! Norman Rockwell will look down from heaven and wish he were still here to paint our story. Right? Hmmm… maybe someone forgot to give the script to all of the players.

The first several weeks went very well. Dad had a list of chores around the house that he could use an extra set of hands to tackle and Mom was happy to have her baby boy back within reach. But the list of chores soon finished, and the "new" wore off of the son, and they wanted to know what we intended to do. They did not need any more help and were afraid we were going to try to take charge of their lives. Although Dad was 85, he was not ready to admit that he could use some help. Okay…this will work…we can spend a few years launching our new business and establishing ourselves in Grand Junction.

Fast forward another year and the phone calls started…

> "Tom, your mom fell in the driveway, and I can't get her up." "Dad it is winter. Do you want to leave her in the driveway while I drive an hour to get to you or do you think you should call an ambulance?" "Well, son, I can get her a blanket. If you hurry, I'm sure we can wait."

> "Tom, we do not have any hot water, and I can't figure out the problem."

> "Tom the ice dammed on the roof, and water is coming in through the living room wall."

> This was a good one. Dad borrowed a small backhoe from his neighbor and his plan was to have Tom lift him in the bucket, so he could stand in it and repair the roof. After all, he's only 88! Nothing

wrong with that plan! After dad realized he couldn't steady himself in the bucket they switched places and Tom (all 280 pounds of Tom) went up in the bucket (small bucket). The Keystone Cops couldn't have done it better. Another opportunity to rely on prayer. Tom is also afraid of heights…not all the language was praise worthy.

> "Tom, are you and Deb coming for dinner? When you get here we can go to that new restaurant in Delta." (50 miles to Cedaredge, 15 miles to Delta, 15 miles back to Cedaredge, 50 miles to Grand Junction = 130 miles to go out to dinner.) The restaurant wasn't that good. Much of the Colorado Highway system is picturesque, towering mountains, rolling rivers and plush green fields with livestock grazing. The majority of the drive between Grand Junction and Cedaredge is brown high desert, flat and ugly.

Tom and I worked on gently easing Mom and Dad off the mountain and down to Grand Junction. We had rented a home near the highway to Cedaredge. We furnished a bedroom for them and partitioned off one part of the house with drapery, so they could have a sense of privacy. When they had a medical reason to come to Grand Junction we encouraged them to spend a few days with us. I cooked their favorite meals and baked goodies. We went to a wide variety of restaurants, played cards at night, recorded programs we knew Mom would enjoy.

After a couple of years, they were spending more time with us and realizing that they felt better when they did. The stress caused by anticipating the next fall or the next task that could not be easily performed was gone. At the entrance to your home town there is likely a sign with a clever slogan and the population. In Colorado, there is a sign with a clever slogan and the elevation. Grand Junction is 2,000 feet lower than Cedaredge. The lower the elevation the easier it is to breathe. Mom and Dad are both on oxygen for COPD, and they noticed they felt better at our elevation.

By the grace of God, Mom and Dad's primary physician retired and they couldn't find another doctor outside of Grand Junction, so they agreed it was time to move. We started looking for a home to purchase together in

Grand Junction. Tom and I would look at several, narrow that search down to 2-3, and then go back to those homes with Mom and Dad. Our Real Estate Agent deserves a crown in heaven!

After months of searching, we walked into a home that accommodated all of our needs. The formal dining room had been turned into a lovely second living room for mom, the third bedroom would work well as an office for dad. The master suite was perfect for Mom and Dad and the guest bedroom was large enough for our king size bed. There were gardens for Dad to putter in and a shop in the garage. Mom sat down in the living room and said, "This is the one." Tom and I moved in first, then Mom and Dad three weeks later. It has been 5 years now. There have been a few Walton's moments and few Hatfield's and McCoy's moments, but all in all it is working.

The first year was the roughest, dad cursed us on a regular basis for taking away his autonomy, and he spent many a Sunday morning perusing the rental section of the newspaper fully prepared to move out. But he didn't and he eventually settled down. Now that he is 93 and Mom is 89, they tell us almost daily how thankful they are that we are there to care for them. Dad has dementia now, so he can tell us how thankful he is every five minutes. Maybe that's God's way to be sure we get enough "thank you" statements to mend the wounds left from the cursings.

Our goal in telling our story is not to give you a blueprint to follow but an outline. Every situation is different; every family is different. If co-habiting is the path you choose we hope you will take the time to plan it out. Our recommendation is to start your plan with a pencil and buy a big eraser. Start with the big picture and work your way down to the little things. You may want to put the final plan in writing and have everyone sign it. Later conversations will go smoother if they start with "Remember when we laid out our family plan? We covered this then." This is also helpful when the relatives visit and try to challenge you. In our case there were no siblings to challenge us or help us (a blessing and a curse). If you have siblings, try to involve them in the process. If not, a pastor and/or an attorney can be helpful. I can tell you that the vision we had for our family was very different than the vision my in-laws had.

Things to work out in advance include:
1. Which part of the house will be your private space? (Trust me, you need this!) Which will be a private space for Mom and Dad?
2. Address finances. You may have to make modifications to your home, from as simple as grab bars to a full remodel. The flooring may need to be replaced to accommodate a walker or wheelchair.
3. Believe me, seniors need their own bathroom. Which leads to…who is going to clean that bathroom when they are no longer able to do it themselves? You think your three-year-old had bad aim at the toilet…let me tell you…
4. Your utility, grocery and transportation costs will increase.
5. What about the last 60 years of precious collectibles, or all of Dad's tools? When my in-laws moved in with us, they brought enough outdated food to feed a small country, plastic wrap to wrap the house, and every time Dad misplaced a tool, he bought another, so he had dozens of everything!
6. Who is going to park their car where?

7. Who will grocery shop, clean, do laundry?
8. Wills, estate planning, funeral plans, living wills, DNR's?
9. What happens if you and your spouse die in a car accident? (Who'd have thought of that one?)

I would tell you about the day we had to take away the car keys, the process to secure and protect their assets, or the time Dad was scammed by a phone call from Bulgaria, but there are other chapters in this book to cover those.

You will likely need help in caring for Mom or Dad. You may not need help in the beginning, but eventually you will. Some families are blessed to have enough members nearby to share the responsibility. It may be your sole responsibility to manage the care of Mom or Dad (or both); and, if you work, you may require the use of an outside agency. We have Visiting Angels in our house, so Tom and I can still work. Visiting Angels can assist you with this care. If your parent has dementia, there are adult day care facilities where you can drop your loved one off in the morning and pick him or her up in the evening. Find someone in your community that is familiar with these resources, like Visiting Angels or a similar agency.

The most important thing to remember is that your parents are still your parents. I have heard the term "Parenting a Parent." I cringe every time. What is happening when we care for our parents is we are "Honoring our Parents." There are certainly some role reversals involved, but it is important to remember that they are your parents. They are from a different era, and they have different values, and expectations than our generations, but they are family. They love us, and we love them (most of the time).

This scenario is not exclusive to Tom and me. If your family is blessed with the gift of longevity you will be faced with these decisions as well. What are your options? Assisted Living facility? Skilled Nursing Home? Secured Dementia Facility? For many of us, and for our parents, these options bring up memories of bad movies, scary stories or painful experiences. We would all love to stay in our own home and pass peacefully in our sleep. The reality is this rarely happens outside of a Lifetime channel movie. With the miracles of modern medicine, we are living well into our nineties and often outliving our functionality. Some of our families are blessed with the means to remain at home with private-duty home care, but this care on a 24-hour basis is outside the financial reach of many. When Tom's parents cared for their own parents, they all lived in a very small town in Colorado. They were only separated by a mile or two. Mom didn't work and she had several siblings to help. This was the norm then; it is not today. We baby boomers have spread out all over the country, and, let's face it, the invention of birth control has made a real dent in the sibling pool. We hope you find our story beneficial.

Good luck and God bless you!

Debbie and Tom Harrison are the owners and directors of Visiting Angels Living Assistance in Grand Junction, Colorado. This chapter was written by Debbie with the invaluable editing assistance of her fabulous son in law Bill Rider. When asked why we take care of Mom and Dad as we do, we often answer by saying, "We are training our children."

Chapter 3- Homecare vs. Facility Life
Gail Lohman

My love for working with seniors started early in life. I was always the kid on the block that helped my aging neighbors take care of their homes and animals and then at 15 I had my first "real" job at an assisted living facility serving residents in the dining room. After college I worked more than 15 years with several organizations representing elderly care facilities throughout my state and then with two young children at home I became a volunteer driver with Meals on Wheels and also volunteered at my church helping seniors. I loved making a difference in the lives of those I helped and saw the direct benefit of helping them in small ways be able to stay in their own homes. All of these experiences taught me not only about aging and working with seniors, but about the options available to seniors as they age.

Seven years ago I first saw an ad for Visiting Angels. I knew about in-home healthcare, which offers licensed medical assistance, but I had no idea companies like Visiting Angels, which offers "non-medical" assistance, existed. Although I wasn't looking to have my own business I knew this was the perfect fit for me and I researched and then subsequently purchased my franchise office in Cameron Park, California.

What I have found as I'm out in our community is that I was not unique – most people do not know about homecare and how it can help their loved ones remain at home. I remember the founder of Visiting Angels, Jeffrey Johnson, told me that he started Visiting Angels when he worked in an elderly care facility and saw how many people moved in but truly wanted to stay at home but didn't have the information or the support to help them. There are wonderful elderly care facilities and I remain an advocate for many in our area. For those that want to remain home, either on their own with family, home care is a wonderful option.

Homecare brings one on one assistance to the senior, allowing them to receive the services needed to maintain their independence and lifestyle in their own home. With some people as little as nine or ten hours a week may be all that is needed to allow them to stay – perhaps helping with showering/bathing, grocery shopping, cooking and cleaning. With others, more time might be needed to assist with dressing, transfers, driving and medication management. Others that are facing the end of their life may need full bed care and/or assistance around the clock.

Whatever the need is– big or small – homecare meets with the needs of the individual by developing an individual plan of care to allow them to stay exactly where they want to be – home. I have seen this over and over throughout my career with my clients but also with my family. Having come from the nursing home industry I know first-hand that there are wonderful options available…and not so wonderful.   It is important to visit any facilities, ask questions and check websites for ratings. It is surprising what you can learn from a Google search! What is most important is making a choice that is right for your loved one.

When your loved one needs help and you are weighing the options of having them remain at home or moving them to a senior care facility there are two main considerations – (1) the type of help and services needed and (2) the cost.

The first step is to determine what level of services are needed. Companion care (ensuring safety, medication reminders, driving, appointments, errands, shopping, etc.); personal care (toileting, showering, bathing, dressing, meal preparation, medication reminders, etc.), and dementia or Alzheimer's care). Families and friends try to fill the needed gaps helping with shopping, errands and personal care but many times the loved ones become overwhelmed with these added responsibilities to their already busy lives. Many times all our loved one needs is just a little help to stay independent and stay at home.

Prices for homecare vary based on the location and services needed but generally fall between $19/hour and $28/hour. Again, depending on your area of the country, and the level of skilled care your loved one would require, facility care could range from $100 to $300 per day. Many people have a mistaken understanding that Medicare will pay for the bills for a loved one to be in a facility. That simply is not the case. The laws, requirements and conditions change on a regular basis, but suffice to say that the care recipient could be left paying for a substantial portion of the facility care bill, until nearly all of their assets are depleted. Beyond that point, Medicaid will partner with families to cover the cost of facility care. That means nearly all of their Social Security check will be used to pay for facility care, and the family choices on what nursing home to use are very limited.

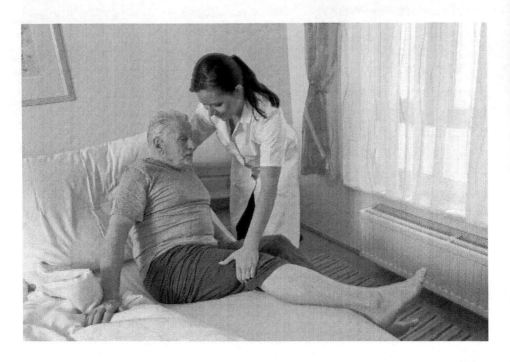

I understand how hard it is to be a caregiver. My own father was always adamant that he be allowed to remain home and he did not want to move to a facility. Several years ago his heart began to fail and he was on hospice care. When I traveled home to see my parents I quickly saw that although my father needed assistance it was really my mother, his primary caregiver that needed help. She was exhausted and overwhelmed and was getting little sleep. We hired caregivers to come each day which gave my father the care he needed so we could honor his choice and keep him home if at all possible. I helped care for him at home and was blessed to be with him when he passed in his own bed with my mom and I by his side.

I have lived this story and have seen from my personal experience how my own family has benefitted from having caregiver support. My own father was able stay in his own home, exactly where he wanted to be. Recently my 90-year-old mother has moved in with my family. Although she doesn't need assistance at this time our plan is the same – to keep her home if at all possible.

For many people homecare may not be an option or perhaps it is preferred. I have seen many wonderful facilities and know that this is sometimes the best solution for senior care. My advice is to do your research, get first hand recommendations; if possible, visit the facilities that interest you in person and ask lots of questions. According to the Genworth 2015 Cost of Care Survey the median cost of a one-bedroom unit in an assisted living facility (room and board, meals and limited personal care) is more than $43,000 per year. For a semi-private room in a nursing facility (room and board, personal care, supervision, medications, therapies with on-site nursing) is more than $80,000 per year. Before making a decision one thing to ask is what is included in the monthly fees.

Many families are caught off guard after moving a loved one into a facility when they find out that many of the personal care services such as bathing, grooming, and medication reminders are "add-on" costs. These "add-ons" can amount to hundreds of additional dollars every month.

Families that budget for facilities many times aren't prepared for these additional costs which can lead to a crisis in care if monies are depleted faster than expected. Another budget buster is planning on one level of care but then because of a change in health or dementia your loved one requires a higher level of care which translates to a much higher dollar amount.

In closing this chapter, I want to say that I understand your story – it is hard being the caregiver. Take care of yourself and you will be able to care for others.

Chapter 4- Managing Meds and Health Issues
Margaret Maczulski

Take Your Vitamins

It used to be so simple; one a day pill for just about everything. Of course your loved one absorbed vitamin D from the milk they drank and vitamin C from orange juice. There were a whole lot of vitamins and nutrients from fruits and vegetables that were beneficial when they ate their meals. Eating those fruits and vegetables is still good for them. For most kids, except for the occasional flu or cold, they required no other medication. There were times when one might need an antibiotic for an infection but it was only for a short duration.

Then They Grew Up

Adults have a whole host of diseases, illnesses and maladies acquired genetically, environmentally, circumstantial and through a series of choices in living. Seniors have even more of a need for supportive medication because it comes with age. Managing what medication their doctors have prescribed is important to them continuing to function as uneventful as possible albeit with the assistance of drugs that are naturally absent in their body. Add to that the supplements and herbal remedies that many feel are important to one's health.

The fact that many people have multiple conditions and multiple doctors makes it all the more important to understand what is being taken, how it is being taken and keeping everyone who is involved in their health administration informed. You and your loved one must be your own advocate to maintain your loved one's well-being. It is very important that medication and dosages are considered a life and death proposition. Take medication seriously and keep all the important people informed of what your loved one is taking and when. Keep a current list of medications at all times handy and easy to refer to should the need arise. Such as:

Medication	Dosage	Time	Time	Doctor	Comments
Name	150 MG/ 1 tab daily	1AM		Dr X	For calm stomach
Name	240 MG/ 1 tab daily	1AM			
	1 tab daily	1AM			
	2 tabs daily	1AM	1PM		
	1 tab daily		1PM		
	1 Drop per eye daily	1AM			
	1 Drop per eye daily		1PM		

Modern day medicine applies science and technology to help the physician to diagnose, treat, and prevent injury and disease, typically through medication or surgery. Medicine has existed for thousands of years, during most of which it was science as well as an art and frequently having connections to the religious and philosophical beliefs of local culture.

To give some idea of the scope of medication today, the list includes but is not limited to the:
- ➢ The digestive system
- ➢ The cardiovascular system
- ➢ The central nervous system
- ➢ The muscle-skeletal disorders
- ➢ The eyes, ears, nose and throat
- ➢ The reproductive and urinary system
- ➢ The skin and infections
- ➢ Pain management
- ➢ Brain and mental disorders
- ➢ Euthanasia

Taking meds can have risks, and dosages are often observed initially for effectiveness. Changes are often made.

So looking at the total picture of your loved one's medication is important and must include the recipient of the medication, their family, their caregiver and each and every health provider who assists them, including their pharmacist. Their eye doctor and their foot doctor need to know what meds they are taking in order to evaluate any condition that brings them into the doctor's office.

According to the American Society of Health Systems Pharmacists, more than 34% of seniors take medications prescribed by more than one physician and 72% take medications that were prescribed more than six months ago. This is one reason why everyone who is involved needs to be aware of the potential for drug interactions.

There may be times when multiple medications are needed to manage symptoms or provide relief in some form. Interactions occur when medications do not work in tandem with one another and instead one of the drugs or both of them together adversely affect your loved one's health. Prescriptions and over-the-counter medication should both be considered when looking at drug interactions. Herbal remedies and food interactions can be a source of concern as well. Drug reactions are just as critical as interactions since they can cause problems for the recipient patient.

One medication can increase or decrease the effectiveness of another. Taking two medications can produce one interaction that can be dangerous to the patient. Taking two medications that are similar can produce one reaction that is greater than the one that is normally expected. Herbal remedies should be considered in conjunction with your prescription medications. Some claim tremendous health benefits but have not been subject to the same level of testing by the Food and Drug Administration (FDA) that pharmaceuticals have been.

Certain foods can also affect medication. Foods can slow the absorption of some medications throughout the body. Meals high in carbohydrates can adversely affect the absorption rate of some medications. Some medications need food in order to be absorbed for the body's use.

The National Institute of Alcohol Abuse and Alcoholism estimates that 25% of emergency room admissions may have alcohol drug interactions as a component of the underlying problem. The elderly are especially at risk for this type of interaction since they consume more than 30% of all prescription medications consumed in the US today and the real risk of alcohol abuse is also significant in the elderly population.

Pain medication has to be taken sparingly and with great caution. Use these types of pills only for the shortest amount of time and the lowest dosage that is effective. They are highly addictive and frequently abused. Similar is the use of sleep medication. Over the counter is promoted heavily as are certain meds on television. The more that these are used, the less effective they become. There are healthy methods, which with some patience will help the sleepless. Ask their doctor, or ask your doctor to recommend a sleep specialist who can analyze their situation and make recommendations.

For the nearly 30 million people who have diabetes, the condition is constant. They may work hard all day to control blood sugar only to have glucose levels go haywire when night falls. Fortunately, simple lifestyle corrections can make the difference along with whatever medication their doctor prescribes. Keep cocktails low-carb. For those on insulin, a glass of wine or a beer with dinner is fine. But too much alcohol can cause blood sugars to drop dangerously while sleeping. Stick to low-carb choices like whiskey, rum and vodka, and indulge in moderation.

Medication for cholesterol is important because diets today have too much saturated fats causing plaque to build up in the arteries leading to heart disease. Medication will help manage cholesterol but it will not "cure" this malady for the 30% of Americans afflicted. Portion control and fruits and vegetables are beneficial but some may need the extra support that a pill will provide. But one has to take it consistently to benefit. This holds true for hypertension, and high blood pressure. It is often called the "silent killer" because there are seldom symptoms for many years. Dangerous levels of blood pressure may cause headaches, chest pains, heart attacks or strokes. THESE COULD BE AN EMERGENCY. A good diet will produce generally good results but a medication might be necessary to regulate their blood pressure.

The government has been heavily involved in the regulation of drug development and drug sales. In the U.S., the Elixir Sulfanilamide disaster led to the establishment of the Food and Drug Administration, and the 1938 Federal Food, Drug, and Cosmetic Act required manufacturers to file new drugs with the FDA. The 1951 Humphrey-Durham Amendment required certain drugs to be sold by prescription. In 1962 a subsequent amendment required new drugs to be tested for efficacy and safety in clinical trials. Until the 1970s, drug prices were not a major concern for doctors and patients. As many more drugs became prescribed for chronic illnesses however, costs became burdensome and by the 1970s nearly every U.S. state required or encouraged the substitution of generic drugs for higher-priced brand names. This also led to the 2006 U.S. law, Medicare Part D, which offers Medicare coverage for drugs.

As of 2008, the United States is the leader in medical research, including pharmaceutical development. U.S. drug prices are among the highest in the world, and drug innovation is correspondingly high. In 2000 U.S. based firms developed 29 of the 75 top-selling drugs; firms from the second-largest market, Japan, developed eight, and the United Kingdom contributed 10. France, which imposes price controls, developed three. The criticisms of Medicare and the costs continue. All this does not count, however, if your loved one does not take their medications as prescribed. That means every day, at the same time, at the correct dosage.

If you have the misfortune of being admitted to the hospital, it can put their daily schedule into a tailspin. When they are discharged to home, take an inventory of all their meds, make a complete list and begin asking questions.

Go to every one of their doctors, even the doctors they may only visit once or twice a year if the doctor has given your loved one an active prescription. This includes drops; creams; pills; tablets and liquids. Give the doctor or their nursing staff your loved one's list and ask them if the prescriptions are OK or if they need to change the quantity or the dosage. Go to the pharmacist's and ask them to review your loved one's prescription profile.

Stay on the schedule that your parent(s) has as to when to take meds. Organize the meds in a 7-day planner (or more elaborate machines) by day and times and keep their medications in a safe, dry place. If they live alone, let someone know where they keep their meds.

When they go to their doctors, bring a copy of their medications for the practitioner to review and make changes as necessary. Ask what the benefit of a specific medication and if there is a lower-cost generic available. Find out if it is OK to split a pill, or take it every other day and still be effective but costing less. How about free samples? Or is there a manufacturer's discount card or program?

Summary

Medication does improve the quality of your loved one's life if they use them correctly. That means to:

> - Keep a schedule. Take them at the same time of day. Make it a habit. And know if the meds are effective with or without food.
> - Keep a complete up to date list that should be reviewed each time they visit any doctor.
> - Also show their medication list to your pharmacists, especially if there has been a change.
> - Keep a list handy for all those who are interested in their welfare.
> - Use a 7-Day Planner for their meds.
> - Keep the pharmaceutical bottles all together in a cool, dry place (unless instructed to keep in the refrigerator).

- ➢ Review all bottles every 3 months and dispose of unused and out of date medication. Disposal should be done correctly. Ask your pharmacist or call your waste disposal company or the local police department as to where to bring out-of-date meds. Do not flush any medication down the toilet or put in the trash.
- ➢ Do not share his or her medication with anyone.

If you have any questions, or you question something about taking your loved ones' medication, always ask. That is your right and you need to be comfortable knowing that what they are taking is safe and beneficial to them. Stay involved and keep your loved one involved as well. After all, that's what medicines are: helpful aides used to maintain health throughout your loved one's lifetime. Medication can be lifesaving if managed well. It is not always easy and not as easy as just taking a daily vitamin.

Chapter 5- Myths in Homecare
Debra Desrosiers

Discharge Today?

Imagine this scenario: you land in a hospital after a fall and are having breathing issues. After a couple days of testing and initial recovery, the nurse informs you that you are being discharged tomorrow. They recommend that you set up 24-hour supervision or be admitted to a rehabilitation facility while you regain your strength. ***What?*** In a flash, your emotions are like a roller coaster and your mind is racing. Moving back and forth between being happy to be released and feeling afraid of what lies ahead, it is understandable how most people become tally overwhelmed, at a time when you've just had a scare in terms of your own mortality.

No one is exempt. Our lives can turn upside down in a matter of seconds. What if you are alone and do not have the capacity or strength to cope with such a decision? Often in these situations, you have very little time to make arrangements, much less know where to look for good care. Hopefully after reading this chapter, you will take the time to set up a plan to have at your fingertips in the event this ever happens to you or your family.

Fact vs. Myth
MYTH- My health insurance will pay for home care services.
Every health insurance plan is unique. Some provide coverage for home care, but many do not.

MYTH- I will have nurses in my home daily after heading home from the hospital.
Most services providing a home visit by a nurse will be limited to once a week to check vitals. If you have wound care, services are typically several times a week.

MYTH- You are guaranteed services at home.
You only receive services when qualified under Medicare guidelines. Many individuals are discharged home and do not qualify for services.

MYTH- Medications will be monitored daily by the home health services.
Medication reconciliations or reviews are done by a nurse upon admission to home health services. However, it is very important to fully understand that it is up to the family or patient to make sure that medications are taken timely and at the right doses.

FACT- Physical Therapy can be provided at home.
Physical therapy can be approved by the physician and can be delivered in the home or at an out-patient facility (for which you would need to arrange transportation). Under Medicare, there are physical therapy services available. More and more home-based programs are becoming available in many areas.

As we review the above "Fact vs. Myth" section, you can see how it is easy to make assumptions that are not rooted in reality, especially when we are in a highly stressed state. It is best not to take what others tell us as reliable truths regarding services. Here is information you can trust as you educate yourself on the facts.

The Call
We often get a desperate call from families who delayed setting up homecare services and now are in a crisis situation. Sometimes families do not recognize how just a few hours a week would have helped to preserve Mom or Dad's safety and independence. Consider these points and remember to be **P.R.O.A.C.T.I.V.E.** **(See definition on next page.)**

P. **PROTECT** Mom or Dad's choice to remain at home by being proactive into looking for resources to assist them to remain as independent as possible.

R. **RESEARCH** your options. Later in this chapter is a complete checklist for your convenience. Look for "Choosing a Homecare Agency with Confidence" which can also be accessed and shared at:
www.homecareofnh.com/blog/blog/choosing-a-homecare-agency-with-confidence

O. **OPEN** your eyes fully to Mom and/or Dad's current status of physical, mental/emotional and cognitive state. Not how it was 20 years ago, but how it is today and knowing they will decline as time marches on.

A. **ASSESSMENTS** by a care manager to fully understand the current situation and future needs of your parents.

C. **CHECK** on what training the caregiver has received. Have they had courses in palliative care, dementia and activities?

T. **THINK** nutrition! Look inside Mom and Dad's refrigerator. Expired food, or very little food is a clear indication that help is needed.

I. **INSIST** on professional care that is insured, which should be in place with a reputable agency. Be sure to ask! Privately hired caregivers can leave the door wide open for a variety of liability risks.

V. **VERIFY** what the options are of a long term care insurance policy or what reserves they have for private pay.

E. **EDUCATE** yourself on dementia. Specific communication methods work well for people with a form of dementia like Alzheimer's disease.

Questions to Ask

We hope this section on homecare services sheds some light on a complex situation. We encourage you to open your eyes so your family can prepare. Research your options. Once you have gathered the information, formulate your plan.

Older adults are more prone to injuries and illnesses. When a tragic event occurs, families scramble to arrange for care options. Do you have a plan? What does it look like? Who would be able to provide care for your loved one? Who is going to pay for it?   If you cannot answer these questions, you need to educate yourself and put a plan in order. It is best to have a plan A, B and C outlined so when it is time to make a decision, you are prepared.

Upon discharge from a hospital or rehabilitation facility, you need to plan accordingly. Inquire how much help will be needed. Consider their mobility; can they walk to the bathroom by themselves or would that present a fall risk? Do they need an assistive walking device? How often do they get up at night and need assistance to the bathroom? How many hours can they be left alone? Do they need 24-hour supervision? Can they prepare a meal on their own? Can they do their own laundry? Can they get in and out of the shower without risk? Can they climb stairs with confidence? Do they remember to turn off the stove and lock the door? Can they use a phone (see and press the right numbers, etc.)?   This and many, many other questions are routine in a good homecare assessment conducted by a professional case manager.

Once you have an initial plan in place, it is time to determine the cost of the plan and how you are going to pay for it. What types of insurance plans are in place? Is there a long-term care insurance policy you can activate and what are the details of the policy? Is there supplemental health insurance coverage, long term care insurance, and disability insurance or life insurance? Find out exactly what is available and covered in terms of financial resources to pay for needed care.

Home Health Care vs. Private Duty Homecare

What is homecare? There are several types of homecare services available. Let's take a look at the differences between choices and review how these services are typically covered.

Home health services are "medically necessary services" and are ordered by a physician. They are typically ordered upon discharge from a hospital or rehabilitation facility. These services are only provided by a Medicare Certified Home Health agency under strict Medicare guidelines. The individual receiving services must remain homebound to receive services under the Medicare benefit. Services must be delivered by licensed professionals. The type of services delivered depends upon the receiver's injuries and illnesses. Care received will be by a nurse, physical therapist, occupational therapist, speech therapist, and/or Licensed Nursing Aid (LNA). These services are only temporary and do not provide consistent help in the home which is called "long term care" or "custodial care".

Home health services are covered under Medicare Part B. Here are some questions to see if you qualify for Home Health services:

> Has the patient had an acute healthcare crisis such as an unexpected illness, injury, surgery, or diagnosis requiring very recent hospitalization?
> Has the patient declined to the point they are homebound?
> Does the illness, injury or diagnosis require treatment, or monitoring following hospital discharge?
> Has the patient declined in functional status following hospitalization? Examples would be weakness, inability to walk or transfer safely, when they were fully functional prior to hospitalization
> Is a chronic illness being managed poorly resulting in repeated hospitalizations, or emergency room visits?
> Does the patient have a primary physician who could write an order for home health care?
> Has the patient just been diagnosed with a chronic illness that needs careful management and education, such as diabetes?
> Is the patient preparing to be discharged from a rehabilitation facility, and is still in need of therapy? Remember, the patient must be homebound.

Examples of skilled home health services include:
> Wound care for pressure sores or a surgical wound.
> Patient and caregiver education for a new illness or diagnosis ex. Diabetes.
> Intravenous or nutrition therapy and injections.
> Monitoring serious illness and unstable health status.

The goal of home health care is to treat an illness or injury. Home health care helps you get better, regain your independence, and become as self-sufficient as possible.

Home health staff should:
> - Check what you are eating and drinking.
> - Check your blood pressure, temperature, heart rate, and breathing.
> - Check prescription, ensure other drugs and any treatments are being taken correctly.
> - Ask if you are having pain.
> - Check your safety in the home.
> - Teach you about your care so you can take care of yourself.
> - Coordinate your care. They must communicate regularly with you, your doctor, and anyone else who gives you care.

Many families expect that continuous help will be offered but are shocked to find out the visits are not written in stone as to the day and time they will arrive at your home. The nurse can only assist with what Medicare regulations dictate and cannot help with anything further while in the home like making them a meal or assisting them with a shower. The visits are typically only 45-60 minutes in length and then they need to leave for their next assignment.

Private duty homecare is also known as "custodial care" or "homecare services" and is non-medical assistance in a home or facility. Services can be highly customized for the actual and changing needs of the family. A physician's order is not needed. The goal of homecare services is to allow the individual to remain independent and safe in their homes. These services range from safety supervision, hygiene or bathing assistance, meal preparation, housekeeping, transportation to medical appointments or errands, light pet care, mental stimulation and joyful companionship, just to name a few. The hours can range from two hours to round the clock care. Homecare services are paid by personal savings, veteran's benefits, Medicaid programs, long term care insurance, or disability insurance.

Consider the following to determine if private duty homecare services are needed:
> - Has there been a recent illness, injury or surgery? Is the individual needing services less functional or independent?

- ➤ Are they unsafe alone?
- ➤ Has there been a noticeable memory loss or a diagnosis of Alzheimer's or Dementia?
- ➤ Is most of their time spent alone, inactive and socially isolated?
- ➤ Has the senior given up their driver's license, yet still wants to get out to shop, visit friends and family, attend religious services, get their hair done or go to events or activities?
- ➤ Is assistance needed for grocery shopping, or getting medications?
- ➤ Does the senior want to remain at home rather than move to a long term care facility?
- ➤ Is the family caregiver exhausted, stressed out and at the end of their rope?
- ➤ Does someone need to take time off work every time the senior has a doctor appointment or medical procedure?
- ➤ Is the senior eating poorly or having difficulty taking the right medications at the right time?

Pitfalls of Hiring a Private Caregiver vs. an Agency Caregiver

Although the costs of using agency caregivers are higher than hiring a caregiver privately, consider the safety and security of your senior. An individual hired privately has not gone through the stringent hiring process that a reputable agency requires including: criminal checks, health screening and training. For a checklist, see "Choosing a Homecare Agency with Confidence" at the end of this chapter. One compelling reason to hire a caregiver from an insured, bonded, and reputable agency is to avoid the risk of the caregiver having an accident in the home and deciding to sue the person who hired them.

Some advantages of using a caregiver from an agency include: the caregiver is covered by the agency in case of an accident; services can be increased or decreased based on the clients' needs; the senior receives one-on-one care and companionship.

Many seniors are reluctant to have a caregiver in their homes. To help ease this transition, the family can take the approach with the senior by being proactive in getting some help at home, the senior may be able to stay in their home indefinitely. Typically, after the initial resistance wears off, seniors will wonder how they ever did it without the help of their caregiver.

Hospice Services
The third type of homecare is *hospice services*. Hospice services are palliative or comfort care services and actually benefit the family as well as the patient. Hospice is delivered by a team. Hospice professionals assist with medical care, pain management, emotional and spiritual support. Services are tailored to the needs and wishes of the patient. Hospice services can be delivered in the home, inside facilities, and hospitals.

Here are some of the top questions when considering hospice services:
> - Has the individual been diagnosed with a terminal illness that has no or limited treatment available?
> - Has the individual completed cancer treatments without any improvement and have run out of options?
> - Has the individual been diagnosed with Failure to Thrive or are experiencing significant weight loss, or a significant decline without any explanation?
> - Has a physician told you or a loved one there is nothing else they can do?
> - Do you need equipment or medications related to a terminal diagnosis that are causing a financial burden?

Services provided under Hospice program:
> - Manages the patient's pain and symptoms.
> - Assists the patient with the emotional, psychosocial and spiritual aspects of dying.
> - Provides needed drugs, medical supplies and equipment.
> - Coaches the family on how to care for the patient.
> - Delivers special services like speech and physical therapy when needed.

- Makes short-term inpatient care available when pain or symptoms become too difficult to manage at home, or the caregiver needs respite time.
- Provides bereavement care and counseling to surviving family and friends.

Choosing a Homecare Agency with Confidence

Make no mistake, choosing the right homecare provider is one decision that requires your full attention as well as your very best research efforts. Not only will a homecare provider be taking care of Mom and/or Dad, but they will be in their home, having access to their life, their health, and their possessions. Here is a checklist to help you compare agencies:

- Are they owned and operated by licensed professionals who fully understand your needs?
- How long have they been in business?
- Are they licensed, bonded and insured?
- Do they only hire experienced caregivers?
- Are their caregivers employed or subcontracted?
- Are they paid "under the table"?
- Is there an extensive reference and national background check conducted on new caregivers?
- Do they continuously and systematically monitor their caregivers?
- Do they provide supplemental care in skilled nursing or assisted living facilities?
- Do they offer a full line of services, such as hygiene assistance, meal preparation, diet and hydration monitoring, light housekeeping, transportation to appointments, errands and shopping, and joyful companionship?
- Are their services customizable in terms of schedule and services to best fit your particular needs?
- Does the agency provide 24/7/365 live phone access to a case manager in case of emergencies?
- What training do they provide/require of their caregivers?

- Do they use a computer profiling testing to screen for honesty, deception, work style, leadership, lifestyle, drive, motivation, intellect and demeanor?
- Do they offer a free home assessment?
- Are they registered with the Better Business Bureau?
- Do they check professional and personal references?
- Are their services customizable allowing you to scale up or down hours based on needs?
- What is their minimum hourly requirement?
- Do they offer a free home assessment after business hours or weekend appointments to accommodate the family?
- Do they offer home safety inspections?
- Are they willing to go to Skilled Nursing Facilities to meet with clients prior to discharge?
- Does the agency provide and require on-going classroom style education to their caregivers or is their training delivered via DVDs?
- How much training do they offer staff, and on what topics?
- Does your agency have a third party company to systematically place random calls to clients doing quality checks?
- Does your agency have a third party company systematically place calls to its staff to ensure they are happy and fulfilled with their employment anonymously and offer feedback?
- Does your agency use technology to have up-to-date recordings of care plan tasks and status changes reported to case managers daily?
- Does your agency have an on-line family portal to view schedules, review invoices and see what tasks and activities happened with Mom and/or Dad each day?

As you move forward in your research, we hope this chapter has shed light on the misconceptions in homecare.

Chapter 6- The Sandwich Generation
Dominique Alvarez

The alarm goes off earlier than I would like but I know there is no time to snooze. My daughter needs to be up, ready and out the door by 7:15am. My son needs to wake up by 7:15am to have time to get adjusted to a new day. He has Asperger's and that makes his day tougher than most. By 8:00am I am trying to get him moving so I can get him to tutoring. This becomes the magic hour for me, because if I can't get him to tutoring I won't have time to stop by my mom and dad's house on my way to work. Now to most people reading this they would say "it is ok, you can stop on your way home from work". What they do not realize is, if I do not stop by before work there is a good chance my mom will be in the same clothes she had on the day before. Her Dementia has advanced to the point she doesn't remember to change her clothes, underwear, or even shower.

My mom is only 68. My dad struggles to help her; at 80 years old he has slowed down quite a bit physically and his memory is starting to diminish as well. I am the mother of two teenagers, one with special needs and chronic health issues. I am the daughter/part time caregiver for my mother with Dementia. I am the Sandwich Generation.

You may have heard this term used and were unsure what it was or if it applied to you. The Sandwich Generation is a generation of people, baby boomers and GenXers, who care for their aging parents while supporting and/or caring for their own children. Dorothy A. Miller coined this term in 1981. [i] At her time she was referring to younger women in their thirties and forties who were taking care of their children, but also having to share their time helping parents, friends, or a part time job. As people have started living longer, the caregiver job does not solely fall on the woman's shoulder, this is felt by both men and women.

The image of the Sandwich Generation can really be best seen as a triangle. There are 3 sides to the role you may now find yourself in; the first being as caregiver, the second is provider of financial support and lastly, you are also providing emotional support. Each side is weighted a little differently and so you may find one of the new roles you play more challenging than another.

The role of caregiver is not an easy one to take on, especially when you are still raising children of your own. Beyond that, the dynamic in the relationship you once shared can change dramatically when you become the caregiver. Your mom or dad, who once was a peer, your role model, the strength of your family is now unable to be that person anymore and is looking to you to be that person for them. This slowly erodes you away from being son/daughter and molds you into caregiver. Moments that may have once been shared together, you now view from the outside because you are responsible for helping get your parent(s) through the day.

This was most polarizing for me when celebrating Thanksgiving, my mom's favorite holiday. As I was milling around the kitchen, cooking, setting the table, etc. I found myself constantly making sure that mom didn't walk out of the house, sitting with her to help her "remember" who she was talking to, and sometimes even reminding her of where she was. By the time we sat to eat, there was no gravy made, the rolls were a little burnt and I was exhausted. But my job wasn't done yet, my mom has forgotten how to use utensils, so conversations went to the wayside as I cut up food, cleaned her hands and shirt, and tried to eat myself. At the end of the day I had to decide whether I wanted to laugh or cry. You may find yourself doing both, a lot. Sometimes separately and sometimes at the same time. The stresses of this role are obvious and it could be easy to get lost in them. But there is also a lot of joy that comes from being able to help. By caring for your parent(s) you allow them to continue to be a participant in their regular life, enjoy family celebrations and live life with dignity.

As we find our loved ones' capacity diminishing they will start to struggle with keeping track of their personal finances. Whether this is paying bills on time, keeping track of money, or ensuring they do not fall prey to financial abuse; providing financial support is another challenging yet critical role. Depending on the situation, you may have had the opportunity to plan ahead for financially supporting your parent(s) but in most cases this comes at us without warning. The burden this creates can sometimes be greater than that of the caregiver.

The makeup of the Sandwich Generation shows us already supporting at least one child under the age of 21[i], to then couple that with the ever increasing cost of living, this new role can cause strains on you that hadn't anticipated. Financial support comes in many forms; you may need to subsidize income to allow your parent(s) to live at home or fund a facility, paying for medical care, or missing hours at your job to ensure that you are where they need you to be. Constantly evaluating how you are fitting into the triangle is critical to making sure you are able to balance both aspects of your life.

The last side of our triangle is Emotional Support. No matter how hard I try, I can never fully put myself in my mom's shoes. I can't begin to imagine how it feels to slowly feel myself disappearing, to be frustrated that I can't find words I once spoke with ease, to be lost in what once was a familiar world. So rather than put myself in her shoes I am there to listen. If she needs to be angry at someone, she can yell at me. If she is sad or confused, I'll try and make her laugh. When she just needs to talk, I can patiently listen. Emotional support can be given in many different ways. And sometimes there is a tendency to try so hard to make it all better that sometimes we miss what our loved one needs. It may be as simple as going for a drive and listening to music, cooking a meal together, reading a book out loud, or sitting and listening.

You're the Sandwich- So Now What?

You've read all of this and realize you are "The Sandwich", so now what? First, stop and take a breath because you can do this. This new life of yours is about balance: balancing jobs, money, time and you are not alone. You've have outlets available to you that will allow you to maintain balance in your life.

> ➢ Senior Centers are a great resource; they offer different day programs, outings and even meals. This is a great way to provide emotional support because you allow your loved one to spend time with their peer group and socialize.

> ➢ Support Groups: There are many support groups out there for children caring for parents, spouses who are providing care, even groups for your loved one to attend. Attending allows you to network with other people in similar situations, learn about resources you may have not known of, and give you some time to breathe and vent.

> ➢ Communication: Your employer or friends may not know what you are juggling behind the scenes, they only see your outside stress. Having an open dialogue with the people in your life offers you support and understanding. You may be surprised by who is in your life going through the same challenge.

> ➢ Financial Planner: Seek out counsel on how to best provide financial support without breaking your own bank. A financial planner can help you with the current day to day help, but also advise you looking to the future and how to maximize what you can do on a long term basis. The financial planner can also help you understand your loved one's financial picture.

> ➢ Insurance: It would be good to look into any Long Term Care Insurance Policy that your loved one may have enrolled in or their spouse. This type of policy would allow you to have in-home caregiving to help alleviate some of the burden you are taking on.

> ➢ Veteran Benefits: If your loved one is a Veteran they may qualify for varying benefits through the Veteran's Administration to offer assistance; whether that is with their medical care, homemaker services, or aid and attendance.

➤ In Home Care: Homecare is a wonderful resource available to families to allow them to lead their regular lives while having the confidence in knowing their loved one is being cared for. It relieves a burden from you and is enriching to your loved one's life.

There will be days you get it all right and then there are the other days. As long as you know you are not doing this alone, there are people to support you, resources to help, and another day to start over. Remember, life is a lot like riding a bike, to keep your balance you must keep moving.

---

[i] Miller, D. (1981). "The 'Sandwich' Generation: Adult Children of the Aging." Social Work 26:419–423.

Chapter 7- Protecting Seniors from Scams
Page Cole

Crime knows no discrimination when it comes to conning people out of their hard earned money. Melba had worked as a teacher for most of her life, and her husband Jim had spent his entire career in a manufacturing plant. Between their salaries they had been able to put aside a nice "nest egg" for their Golden Years of retirement. Suddenly that was all in jeopardy.

Melba had been fooled by a kind sounding voice on the other end of the telephone. The sweet young man had reminded her of her own grandson as he described a fresh new investment plan for seniors. He explained how it could double their portfolio in only a few years. All he needed to do was to set up the accounts, and once the investment fund was linked to their cash account, Melba and Jim could move as much or as little money into the new investment account. That's what he told her, but it was a lie.

She was excited when Jim came in from playing golf, and wanted to show him the new financial tool she had signed them up for. As she logged on to their bank account online, she was stunned to see that one of their "nest egg" accounts had been totally emptied. As she stared blankly at the screen, she covered her mouth with her hand, and her eyes brimmed with tears. "How could I have been so foolish?" she cried to her husband. "I trusted a complete stranger! What are we going to do?" This scene has repeated itself thousands of times over with seniors across the country.

Data from a recent survey, sponsored by the University of Waterloo, indicated that the percentage of victims of scams and fraud in an age group peaks in late middle age and then declines as people get older. That being said, seniors as a group tend to be a greater target for many reasons. Among those reasons are:

Shame
Seniors tend to allow shame and embarrassment to keep them from sharing how they were scammed with family, friends or law enforcement;

Vulnerability
Seniors are more vulnerable than young adults, especially if they have become widowed;

Passive
The elderly tend to be much less likely to try to fight back than median age or younger adults;

Sensory Issues
Since seniors are more likely to have trouble with their hearing or sight, they can be more easily fooled;

Mental Faculties
With age and the possible onset of various health conditions, their thought processes may not be as sharp. This is even more dangerous if the senior has experienced the onset of any form of dementia;

Effects of Aging
They are less able to protect themselves both physically and emotionally;

Danger of Injury
Injuries to the elderly are more likely to be very serious or life threatening;

Desperation
With limited or fixed incomes and a tough economy, many senior's level of desperation pushes them to take risks they might not normally take with their finances;

Detachment
It is easy for seniors to feel neglected or detached from busy family members; they become very receptive to the suggestions or direction of others who will pay them attention or spend time with them;

Technologically Disadvantaged
Seniors tend to be less technologically savvy and are more like to be tricked with online scams.

Increased Assets
Seniors tend to have larger cash reserves and resources, making them a much higher priority as a target for scammers.

Sweepstakes & Contests
An AARP study noted that seniors place themselves at a greater risk for being a victim of fraud by doing seemingly innocent things like entering drawings, contests and sweepstakes for the promise of free trips, vacations or prizes; attending free seminars; sitting through time share or others sales pitch meetings; and reading and accepting junk mail offers.

Why Are the Elderly Less Likely to Report Scams?
So why do seniors who have been scammed fail to immediately contact family and/or the authorities? You might assume that most people would want their money back. Aren't they interested in doling out justice to the liars who have taken advantage of them? Typically, seniors fail to report these kinds of scams to anyone. The reasons for this failure to respond vary.

Fear of Family Perception

More often than not, seniors tend to worry about what their family might do if they find out. Grown children can react or overreact by grossly limiting or even removing their parent's access to their own money. Although this may very well be in the senior's best interest, it can be both frightening and humiliating for the senior.

Self-Blame

Defrauded seniors also blame themselves for what happened. Remember, this senior has been a productive and thoughtful member of society. They have held down jobs, raised families and volunteered in their community. No one is more disappointed in them than they are themselves. They might even adopt the belief that they deserve what they got, for not paying more attention or being more discerning.

Pride

Personal pride may also play a part in their response to being scammed. Seniors may believe that they are smart enough or savvy enough to get their money back on their own without any assistance from others. As seniors age, their control of so much of the different areas can slip away- their health, driving ability, even finances. For many this is a matter of life long pride. "I got myself into this pickle, so I can get myself out of it," is their mantra.

Scammers are Relatives

Sadly, many scammed seniors are related to or have a prior relationship with the person who scammed them. When it is a loved one, friend or business acquaintance that has scammed them, they may determine that the relationship is more valuable to them than the assets are. In deference to keeping the relationship with a nephew, neighbor or friend, they will just keep quiet and take the loss.

Fear

Another reason seniors may stay silent about their loss is that they are afraid the person who scammed them might retaliate. This is a very real concern for seniors who have become feeble or dependent upon others for the most basic needs of life. This scenario is more likely the case when intimidation was a part of the initial scam. Seniors who have been scammed would rather face the fear of lost money than the retaliation of the scammer.

Uncertainty about Legal System

The prospect of going through the court system and dealing with lawyers, law enforcement and judges scares many people, and seniors are no different. Seniors face unknown or unrealistic fears about what new legal fees they might face. With investment schemes, there may even be concerns on the part of the senior that they themselves might have a legal problem.

Embarrassment

Do not forget, many seniors are totally embarrassed about what has happened to them. This is by far the most prominent reason seniors fail to report scams and frauds. They can't believe that they were gullible enough to lose so much money. They certainly do not want others to look down on them or ridicule them for this failure, so instead they just stay silent.

Worry About Housing

If the victim is a resident of a nursing home, assisted living facility or retirement community, they may fear they would get kicked out of their home. Again, this may have been an intimidation tactic employed by an employee of the facility who scammed them, or simply a seed of fear planted in their mind by the scammer.

Ignorance

Believe it or not, some seniors are unaware that what happened to them was a crime. As strange as that may seem, some seniors may not understand the criminal nature of the fraud that has been committed against them.

Resignation to Failure

Finally, some will fail to report the crime simply because they are afraid that there aren't enough facts to prove they were scammed. No one goes into one of these situations believing or expecting that they are being scammed.

With an attitude of trust, and feelings of excitement about this new endeavor, many times well-meaning and intelligent seniors may not be as focused on details and record keeping as they should be. As a result, there are verbal contracts, handshakes and gentlemen's agreements, rather than documented paperwork and legitimate contracts.

The AARP regularly studies issues related to seniors and fraud topics. Their studies reflect that many seniors who are telemarketing fraud victims do not understand that the sweet sounding young man who just called them could be planning on stealing their life savings.

The National Consumers League's National Fraud Information Center constantly monitors issues regarding scams and fraud across the country. They estimate that of all telemarketing fraud victims, nearly 1/3 of them are over 60 years old.

It is just not safe or prudent in this day and age to assume that anyone trying to "sell you up" or "sign you up" is honest; quite the contrary. Seniors would like to believe that voice on the other end of the line belongs to a nice young man or woman simply trying to make an honest day's wage. If they are too pushy or seem too confrontational, seniors would tend to believe the best of them anyway. The nice young man on the phone might seem to "stretch the truth" just a bit; many will still err on the side of trust rather than caution.

Of course, the telemarketing industry has a large number of honest and trustworthy people working in it. Still, there are those wolves in sheep's clothing lying in wait for unsuspecting senior citizens. Without losing one bit of sleep, crooks will bilk them out of hundreds or even thousands of dollars. Unlike a gun toting mugger in a dark alley, these thieves use a phone as their weapon of choice. It is very dangerous and devastating to trust too much.

Thousands... yes thousands of deceptive telemarketing companies are open for business daily, according to the FBI. Beyond our borders, there are thousands more around the world who intentionally target U.S. residents from locations as close as Canada and as far away as Nigeria, India and Russia.

Given the global scope and the constant barrage of financial assaults on seniors, help them out by suggesting, educating and equipping them with the following suggestions.

Help Them Understand Their Vulnerability

Seniors haven't always been old... and they haven't always been as vulnerable as they are now. They need to be educated in a way that helps them become aware and guarded, while at the same time maintaining their integrity and self-esteem. Many believe that it is only the lonely, isolated or foolish seniors that fall prey to scams. Nothing could be further from the truth.

Retired teachers, physicians and a variety of well informed and educated professionals fall prey to the tricks of scam artists every day. AARP research reveals that it is many of these typical victims who are successful people are simply tempted by allure of phony promises of amazing deals to grow their retirement "nest eggs." Scammers, unscrupulous telemarketers and con artists take full advantage of that. If it sounds unbelievable, easy and profitable, it is safer to just stop at the word "unbelievable."

We all want to believe that dreams can come true! We all hope someday we will get that call from Publisher's Clearing House, or see our stock choices take off overnight! Many seniors have worked hard, and it is easy to be convinced that their day has come. Family members are shocked when seniors react with frustration or anger if their optimistic response to a scam is questioned.

Seniors come from a generation where courtesy is always in style. Many seniors would NEVER consider hanging up on someone; they believe even strangers deserve their courtesy. Scammers know this, and manipulate the good will and traditional heart of the Greatest Generation and Baby Boomers to their advantage.

Remind them that it is hard to discern who is really honest. Building a good relationship, creating an atmosphere of urgency, building excitement, building a sense of "need" in the senior- these are the tactics of both great salespeople and criminal shysters as well.

Warn them that the power of consistent pressure is overwhelming. Just check the mailbox of the typical senior. It is FULL of junk mail offering deals on property for sale, offers to work from home and get rich, and "add to your nest egg" offers. The numbers of scams thrown at seniors is mind boggling.

Discourage immediate trust from being the natural reaction. Giving someone the benefit of the doubt is the normal reaction for most seniors.

They sound nice, they seem nice, so the person on the other side of the phone must BE nice, or so they believe.

Recognizing The Warning Signs of Fraud

So how do you help seniors be aware of the signal fires of fraud? How can we equip them to spot the tell tail markers of typical scammers? Here are a few suggestions. Look out for:

> - People who refuse to stop calling
> - People who demand payment
> - Promise of Easy Money
> - Requests for Account Numbers
> - Pressed for Immediate Response
> - Scare Tactics
> - Requests to Wire Money
> - Upfront Fees Expected
> - No Information Provided
> - Payment for Information Alone

Signals Seniors Are Victims or at Great Risk

The following signals may alert loved ones and friends that they may have already fallen prey to a scam. Here are the top ten ways you can Pay Attention and protect yourself or your loved ones! Pay Attention to these signals!

Large or Increasing Subscriptions

Pay attention if you see a large number of magazine or book club subscriptions.

Increase in Incoming Phone Calls

If the senior has seen a pick-up in number of phone calls regarding donations to charity or touting special offers, they may be the target of one or more scammers.

Struggling to Pay Normal Bills

Pay attention if you become aware that they are struggling to pay their normal bills, buy gasoline and food or pay their utilities.

Obvious or Suspected Fraudulent Charges

Pay attention by taking immediate action if you become aware of potential fraud. Cancel credit cards or close bank accounts if you feel like they have or may have been compromised by scammers or thieves.

Odd New Products

Pay attention if you notice odd new products around the home. Con artists will take advantage of seniors by luring them in with "instant wins" of smaller items, with the hope of scoring the big prize later. The only problem is that there is never any big prize later, only a discouraged senior and an empty bank account.

Increased Sweepstake/Contest Mail

Pay attention if the senior has seen an increase in sweepstakes, prize and contest mail and email. Mail and sweepstakes fraud are one of the easiest way these criminals take advantage of seniors!

Financial Recovery Specialists

Pay attention if you become aware that "financial recovery specialists" are contacting the senior. If they are contacted by individuals or companies promising to recover money lost to fraud, especially if they want to charge a fee for this service, may actually be scammers themselves.

Strange or Repetitive Payments

Pay attention if you become aware that they have started making consistent and repetitive payments to strange companies. It is especially dangerous if those companies are located out of state or out of country. Be very cautious about phone calls that have unusual 2 digit numbers at the beginning- these are international calls, and once your money or information has crossed the borders of the USA, it is gone for good.

Tension between Senior & Family/Friend

Pay attention if you sense tension between a senior and either a friend or family member regarding finances. It could be that a loved one has actually preyed on the senior and abused the relationship for financial gain. Money issues among family members should be transparent and documented to avoid conflict.

Scammers Repeatedly Abuse Phone

Pay attention by changing the phone number if scammers repeatedly contact the senior, or won't stop calling back. In addition, do not hesitate to contact the authorities and turn the number in to them for harassment and potential elder abuse.

Remember These Important Facts!
Ask a Lot of Questions

If there is a new person or company in the picture, then ask about them, and ask for details... Ask for lots of details. You may not ultimately have any choice in whatever decisions are made, but awareness is the best tool available to limit damage from scams.

Get a Second Opinion

Entire life savings have been wiped out by "trusted advisors" who have taken charge of a senior's finances. Always encourage seniors to seek out a second opinion as a way of offering a second set of eyes on a potential investment.

Have Regular Reviews

Ask for regular reviews of financial investments, quarterly if possible. This allows you to have a consistent base line, and provides regular accountability.

Report Criminal or Unethical Activity

The best way to prevent future scams is to report on those who perpetrate them, and assist in their prosecution in any way possible. Encourage anyone who has been scammed to talk to law enforcement and follow through with prosecution.

Do Your Own Research

Remind seniors that it is empty trust to believe that the government or other business entities have researched and cleared all telemarketing companies, home repair companies or financial planners.

Contact the Law When Necessary

Scammers and unscrupulous vendors will only be stopped from doing further damage if they are arrested and punished. For that to happen, victims of these crimes must put aside their shame, guilt or embarrassment and report these to law enforcement and to consumer protection agencies.

Hire & Use Trusted Companies

Resist the temptation to hire workers directly, outside the direction of the company they work for. In some instances, this is a breach of contract for the employee or the individual. Regardless, the senior runs a significant risk since individual workers have no accountability, and may not be covered by necessary insurance.

Ten Laws of Protection for Seniors

Law of Pay to Play
When asked to purchase something for the chance to win, JUST SAY NO!

Law of No Numbers
Your personal info is the key to your financial life. If someone asks you for your account numbers or SSN over the phone, JUST SAY NO!

Law of Not Now
If challenged or pushed to sign any number of legal or financial documents, while discouraging you from getting a second opinion, JUST SAY NO!

Law of Second Opinions
Always seek the advice and perspective of financial and legal counsel when considering spending, investing or committing large sums of money. If pushed to press ahead without seeking such counsel, JUST SAY NO!

Law of Face to Face
Absolutely refuse to conduct business over the phone, unless you have gone to a website or your bill/paperwork, and initiated a call to them. If someone calls you and demands you do business during their call, JUST SAY NO!

Law of License Only
Do not hire home repair contractors, especially those offering to do repairs after a storm, unless they are local and offer you a verifiable copy of their license. JUST SAY NO!

Law of "Pros Know"
Secure your financial future by using a reputable elder estate attorney or financial planner. From anyone else who offers, JUST SAY NO!

Law of Show Me Your Badge
You do not owe it to anyone to let them into your home. Demand ID from anyone doing a home inspection. If they refuse, JUST SAY NO!

Law of No Fear

Do not be afraid of intimidation or speculation. If someone uses scare tactics about dangers in your home to get you to commit to repairs, JUST SAY NO!

Law of No Withdrawal

If someone wants you to withdraw large amounts of money for a purchase or any other reason, JUST SAY NO!

Contact Information
National Fraud Information Center

Phone: 1-800-876-7060

This is the best consumer resource for reporting telemarketing fraud and report suspicious activity on the Internet. Individuals may also submit complaints online. This is organization is a partnership of the National Association of Attorneys General and the Federal Trade Commission.

Federal Trade Commission Consumer Response Center

CRC-240

Washington, DC 20580

Phone: Toll-free 1-877-FTC-HELP (382-4357) or

1-877-ID-THEFT (438-4338)

Chain Letters

Chain letters used to be much more prevalent than they are today, but they still circulate in a variety of forms even now. If you know a senior who you feel has fallen victim to a chain letter scam, have them send that information to:

United States Postal Inspection Service

Criminal Investigations Service Center

Attn: Mail Fraud

222 S Riverside Plaza   Suite 1250

Chicago, IL 60606-6100

There are three criteria for an illegal chain letter:
If the letter asks for money; OR if there is an element of misrepresentation;
OR if the letter purports that you can expect to receive sums of money.

Junk Mail
Mail Preference Service
Direct Marketing Association
1120 Avenue of the Americas
New York, NY 10036
Phone: (212) 768-7277
Fax: (212) 302-6714

Mail Fraud
U.S. Postal Inspection Service
1745 Stout Street, Suite 900
Denver, CO 80299-3034
Phone: (303) 313-5320
Toll-free: 1-800-372-8347
Fax: (303) 313-5351

A fantastic guide for spotting and protection against mail fraud is available on-line at http://www.usps.com/cpim/ftp/pubs/pub300a_print.htm.

Federal Law – CAN-SPAM Act of 2003
Congress passed the "Controlling the Assault of Non-Solicited Pornography and Marketing Act" ("CAN-SPAM Act") in 2003. It is designed to deal with spam & junk e-mail messages delivering either a commercial offer or pornographic images. CAN-SPAM Act prohibits transmission of any e-mail that contains false or misleading header (or "from" line) information and prohibits false or misleading "subject" line information.

For more info on spam & junk e-mail can be found at
www.ftc.gov/bcp/menus/consumer/tech/spam.shtm

Chapter 8- Family Caregiver Burnout
Valerie Hentzschel

The Caregiver Action Network (caregiveraction.org) reports that there are over 65 million people in the U.S. who currently provide some kind of care for a chronically ill, disabled or elderly family member. This care amounts to an average of twenty hours per week (National Alliance for Caregiver Collaboration with AARP, Nov. 2009). As our society continues to live longer life spans, this number has nowhere to go but up. More and more families will be tasked with the need to be a caregiver or see that someone they love is cared for, a fact making this topic all the more relevant. It is my hope that this chapter will help family caregivers prevent burnout before it starts, identify the signs and offer suggestions and resources to help cope with burnout.

During my 15-year career as a county social worker it is easily said that I encountered this problem on an almost daily basis. The problem at its worst would sometimes show up in an elder abuse report. Take the case of Miss Nancy. She was an elderly woman who lived with Ann, her granddaughter. Miss Nancy originally came to live with Ann after she had a fall in her small mobile home, which resulted in her being unable to get up or get help for several hours. At first Miss Nancy's granddaughter was happy to have her grandmother living with her and did everything she could to make sure Miss Nancy had all that she needed. Ann cooked, cleaned, changed Miss Nancy's sheets and helped her get to the rest room and shower. But after a time Ann had to return to work and so left Miss Nancy home alone during the day. When she returned from her job, Miss Nancy would be in need of many things. Ann assisted her despite beginning to feel overwhelmed and tired. Time wore on and Ann became more and more overwhelmed and resentful. She began to yell at Miss Nancy, have a few drinks in the evening and soon she did not care if Miss Nancy ever got a shower or had a meal during the day. Thus the situation deteriorated. I became involved with Miss Nancy and Ann when an elder abuse report was made by a neighbor who heard yelling next door.

When I arrived I found Miss Nancy alone, unable to get out of bed and not having anything to eat for most of the day. Her granddaughter was at work. I later spoke with both Miss Nancy and Ann. I found, to no surprise, that Miss Nancy's granddaughter was completely overwhelmed. She was tearful and admitted that she did not know how to handle the care needs of her grandmother and her own responsibilities. Ann had few outlets other than her job and no other family members to assist her. She also felt an overwhelming obligation to care for Miss Nancy "all by herself." I tell this story not to say that all family caregiver's end up being abusive, not even to say that most do, but to give an example of how burnout, left unrecognized, can progress to a detrimental level for both care recipient and caregiver. As we look at the case of Nancy and Ann what can we learn about preventing burnout, recognizing the signs of burnout and finding resources and ways of coping?

The best way to prevent burnout is first to resist the idea that you are an "Island". Accept the fact that you will need help and a strong support system. What you have taken on is both admirable and overwhelming. It is easy to get trapped in the idea that you must do everything yourself. We all care for and feel responsible for our loved ones. But we need to remember to take time for ourselves, continue to see friends and family and enjoy some of our favorite activities.

Another thing you need to do to prevent burnout is to be prepared and educate yourself regarding resources that are available to assist with your loved one's care. I often find that families just do not know what kind of help they need and what options they have. For example: does your loved have insurance that will help cover the costs of care? Do you know what agencies are available to help? Does the care recipient need a walker or wheelchair to help make them more independent? Make a list of questions and do your research.

Lastly, give yourself a break. Accept the fact that this would take an emotional toll on anyone in your position. Your loved one needs you in ways that were not there before. In some cases, roles have reversed. You are in the "parent" role and they need you.

So, how can a family caregiver tell when they are over-stressed? Although this is not meant to be an exhaustive list, check yourself related to these 10 signs: Denial, anger, social withdrawal, anxiety, depression, exhaustion, sleeplessness, irritability, lack of concentration, and personal health problems (caregiveraction.org).

Ask yourself a few questions. Do you feel like you have to do it all by yourself? Do you withdraw from activities you used to enjoy and friends you used to see? Do you worry that the person you care for is safe? Do you feel anxious about money and healthcare decisions? Do you feel grief or sadness that your relationship with the person you care for is not what it used to be? Do you get frustrated and angry with the person you care for? Are your own health problems taking a toll on you? (Caregiver Stress Check, alz.org). If you are noticing these signs in your life you need to see them as a wake-up call. They are your body and mind's way of telling you that you are overwhelmed and you need to make some changes.

Once you recognize that you are stressed you need to find ways of coping. Start by reminding yourself that you are doing your best. The difference you make in your loved one's life has value beyond what can be measured. You also need to manage your stress. Use whatever activities you enjoy (e.g. exercise, sports, journaling, hobbies) as an outlet for coping. Be realistic; there are a lot of things you cannot control so enjoy the good times you have with your loved one. It is also very important to give yourself credit. It is normal to lose patience sometimes. We all fall short of perfection.

Look into getting respite. There are agencies, such as Visiting Angels, that can give you a break as well as temporary placements in a facility. Lastly, accept change. Your loved one's condition and needs will change. For example, he/she may go from being able to use a walker to becoming more and more wheelchair dependent. We all want our loved one's condition to improve and this may also be the case. But, whatever the case, change is inevitable. You will need to accept this and go with the flow of changing care needs (some information provided by caregiveraction.org). Everyone has different coping mechanisms. The important thing is that you recognize stress and develop healthy outlets for yourself.

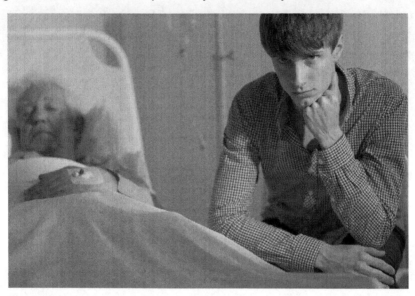

Resources

The last section I would like to cover is resources. I made some suggestions in the previous section, but want to further emphasize some things. In our information age I find it interesting that many family caregivers do not know what's out there. It plays in to the idea that they are so overwhelmed they do not know where to start. I could list dozens of resource groups here, but in the interest of brevity and not knowing every community, I would like to suggest that you start by looking for a support group in your local community. A lot of them are diagnosis specific, such as: Alzheimer's or Parkinson's disease. You can look on the web to find a local chapter and support group. There are also programs for caregiver support through your local Area Agency on Aging that may not be diagnosis specific.

It is also important to understand what your loved one qualifies for under their health coverage. He or she may qualify for temporary respite or home health services, all of which can give you some extra support.

As I mentioned before, let us not forget private duty services like Visiting Angels. Private duty along with Home Health and other services can make a great team.

One other resource near and dear to me, is the assistance of a Social Worker. As your loved one leaves a hospital or rehab part of the plan should include some follow up by a social worker. Home Health agencies also have social work services. Part of a social worker's job is to know and understand local resources and to help you get the services and support you need. If you use all of the tools available to you, you can have the care your loved one needs and the support you need.

It is my hope that you found this chapter and its information useful. To review, remember to educate yourself about resources as well as your loved one's condition and needs, find a support group, get some respite, give yourself a break as you are human and enjoy the activities that provide stress relief for you. Also, remember to do a stress self-check using the caregiver stress check questions from alz.org.

As you think back to that very large statistic that we started with and remember the real life story of Nancy and Ann, it should be easy to see that family caregivers are a large part of the U.S. population. Thus, they are not each his or her own "island", but in fact a "village." So, in closing, I say reach out to your local village.

Chapter 9- Addressing the Signs of Dementia
Debra Desrosiers

"Hey Gram, did you notice you have your pants on backwards?" I asked. She looked down at her outfit, "Oh really? I thought they felt kind of funny today!" We proceeded to laugh together and then corrected the problem. Is this a sign of dementia? You bet it is! As a matter of fact this was an actual conversation between my grandmother and me!

Sometime later, my grandfather called me frantically stating something was not right with Gram and asking me if I could come over. I left immediately. As I entered their home, Gram was giving a piano lesson to a student. Gram called out, "Hello! I will be with you shortly." As I watched her, I observed how she was attempting to give her student a lesson but was fumbling with the music sheets and losing her train of thought. My grandmother taught piano lessons for over 50 years and was very good at what she did. Her students loved her. Was her fumbling with the music sheets as she tried to teach a lesson a sign of dementia? Absolutely.

Gram was a very social lady. She taught approximately ten to fifteen students a week. She gave piano lessons until she was in her mid-80s. Gram also played piano in nursing facilities as a volunteer. The phone call from my grandfather was a reaction to noticing a sudden change in her cognitive status. We knew we needed to address this immediately as a family with her primary care doctor.

When we met with her doctor, we discovered that Gram was being treated for frequent urinary tract infections. She was being taking a strong antibiotic called Ciprofloxacin (Cipro), a medication that should not be given to those with dementia. The primary care doctor did not diagnose or know she had dementia and neither did we. Gram's dementia came on suddenly in her late 80s. She had a history of mini-strokes and was later diagnosed with Vascular Dementia and Alzheimer's disease.

I start with this story because we, as a family, did not notice the signs or symptoms of dementia with my grandmother. Every person is unique and the progression of dementia takes many forms. Many families will hide events going on and attribute them to old age when in fact dementia is not a normal part of aging. Dementia, in its many forms, is a disease that needs to be accurately diagnosed and properly treated. In looking back, I can now recognize the red flags that could have alerted our family to her changing cognitive status.

As the owner of a busy homecare agency, the phone calls come in regularly from frustrated families who are uneducated on how to care for someone with a cognitive problem. This constant flow of calls revealed an obvious need for a "nuts and bolts" style of training that could flex and bend to fit the needs of the learner, including professionals in the field as well as family members. The Caregiver Keys were developed to educate all caregivers on the information they need to navigate this most challenging terrain.

There are six modules to address the different aspects of the dementia journey.

- ➢ **Foundation** – Understand the disease & diagnosis process
- ➢ **Roles** – Develop your support team
- ➢ **Environment** - Learn the systems to put in place
- ➢ **Communication** – Discover a new way to relate
- ➢ **Activities** – Improving quality of life through activities
- ➢ **Survival** – The importance of your respite plan

We will focus on the Foundation key as it is the subject of this chapter. For more information, see www.caregiverkeys.com.

Foundation

I received a call at my office from the wife of a gentlemen in his 60s. As she told her story, she couldn't help crying. She was overwhelmed with news they had received from their primary care doctor just a few days ago. Her husband was having sudden memory issues and had gone to his doctor. The doctor said it was most likely Alzheimer's disease. They were devastated with the news and didn't know where to turn. The wife was referred to me for assistance. I immediately told her to take a deep breath and explain to me what she told her doctor and then asked her what testing the doctor did. She was a bit stumped and said, "Testing?" I immediately knew she was unaware of the protocol for getting a proper diagnosis of dementia and explained the process to her. After hearing my information, she immediately called the doctor and followed my suggestions. She was now armed with important information to help her husband get a proper diagnosis and had some hope.

A few weeks later she called me and thanked me for the help I offered and informed me her husband was diagnosed with a brain tumor and was scheduled to have it removed the following day. Although they still had to deal with a different health crisis, she was relieved. Her husband could have had a much different outcome if they had accepted what the doctor initially told them and that tumor had been undiagnosed and continued to grow.

I share this story because as we do assessments with families and ask the question, "What type of dementia are they diagnosed with?" Many families cannot answer that question. They state, "They have dementia." Or, "I didn't know there were different types." We then begin to educate them on the definition of dementia.

The Dementia Umbrella

It is widely known that cancer is an umbrella term under which there are many different forms; breast, skin, prostate and many other kinds of cancer. Each has their own treatment plans. The same is true of dementia. Dementia is a general term for loss of memory and other mental abilities severe enough to interfere with daily life. Dementia is caused by the loss of or damage to neurons in the brain. Dementia is not a disease but a term used to describe the overall symptoms. There are many types of dementia. The two most common types are Alzheimer's and Parkinson's disease. In most cases, there is no cure. Several types of dementia are reversible as is the case in the previous story of the man with a removable brain tumor.

The most common forms of dementia are:

> - Alzheimer's disease
> - Vascular dementia
> - Lewy Body dementia
> - Mixed dementia
> - Parkinson's disease
> - Frontotemporal dementia

Here are the 10 early signs and symptoms from The Alzheimer's Association:

> - Memory loss that disrupts daily life
> - Challenges in planning or solving problems
> - Difficulty completing familiar tasks at home, at work or at leisure
> - Confusion with time or place
> - Trouble understanding visual images and spatial relationships
> - New problems with words in speaking or writing
> - Misplacing things and losing the ability to retrace steps
> - Decreased or poor judgment
> - Withdrawal from work or social activities
> - Changes in mood and personality

The Alzheimer's Association is an organization that assists with all forms of dementias not just Alzheimer's disease. Their website is very informative with a lot of valuable tools such as the PDF downloadable document "Doctor's Appointment Checklist". You can also keep a notebook journaling the changes and events of a loved one that occur to discuss with your physician. See more details at www.alz.org. A typical sign to watch for is misplacing an item and not knowing where we put it. Although this can happen to any of us, someone with a cognitive impairment is unable to retrace their steps back to the lost item.

The Diagnosis Process

When we start seeing changes in loved ones, it is never easy to accept that change and start to plan for the future. Some families are relieved once they know what the problem is. They can then start to take the appropriate steps to help their loved one remain safe and get the education families need to handle the journey ahead.

The first step of the diagnosis process is to get a complete medical evaluation by the primary care physician. The patient should be accompanied by a trusted family member on all medical appointments to get a clear picture of the situation. The physician's examination will vary depending on their field of expertise and could be very limited. In most cases, the next step will be to get a consultation with a specialist such as a geriatrician, neurologist, or geriatric psychiatrist. A full team comprised of the above specialists is my recommendation. The Alzheimer's Association recommends:

> A thorough medical history
> Mental status testing
> A physical and neurological exam
> Tests (blood and brain imaging) to rule out other causes of dementia-like symptoms

Once all the testing is completed, the professionals can accurately diagnose which type(s) of dementia your loved one has. In some instances, it may be a reversible dementia which can be treated and cured with a proper treatment plan. These include:

> Depression
> Vitamin deficiencies
> Medication side effects
> Excess use of alcohol
> Thyroid problems
> Normal pressure hydrocephalus

Now What?

Once accurately diagnosed, families should begin to plan out what the future will look like. Many doctors sometimes believe they are failing families because there is no cure. They entered the healthcare arena to cure and treat their patients and unfortunately when diagnosing most forms of dementia, they believe they are giving them a death sentence. Because of this, I see many physicians just follow the patient and do not give them many resources to help them cope and manage the disease. Not all, but the majority of doctors could provide more assistance to families, at least in terms of pointing them in the direction of helpful resources as found at the end of this chapter.

I frequently hear that physicians recommend their patients get socially and physically active, eat well and start them on a medication to help them with delaying the progression of the disease as well as quality of life. Every individual with the disease is different and so are the results of taking medications. Most have side effects. You should thoroughly review medications with your physician in terms of interactions with medications the individual is already taking.

The physician may also recommend updating your advance directives and putting a long term plan into place for care and safety. It is very important to include the person diagnosed in all decisions being made. They are still a person with feelings and understand more than many families realize.

Your new "job"

> ➤ Help them to have an active and meaningful life
> ➤ Full acknowledgment that it is the family, not the diagnosed patient, who are the ones who will have to change
> ➤ Understand this journey is different for everyone including the patient, the family, and their extended support network
> ➤ The journey and progression is unique to each patient and their families

World Awareness Needed

I will finish this chapter with a true and jaw dropping story. Mary would occasional call my office asking for prices on transportation because she needed groceries. We would explain our rates and she would politely say, "Oh, that is too expensive, thank you" and would hang up. Everyone in the office got to understand her and we all knew she must have a memory issue as sometimes she may call multiple times not realizing she just called.

One cold January day in New Hampshire, Mary called us. The conversation was different this time. Mary said she was very cold. Our weather tends to be well below freezing that time of year. Knowing she had a memory issue, I asked if Mary if the heat was on. She didn't know. My instinct was that this lady was in trouble so I asked Mary if it would be okay if we could come to her home and look into the problem for her. She agreed and gave me her home address. I asked one of my case managers if they would check into the issue. Once the case manager arrived and looked into the situation, she called our office to report a serious situation.

Mary was a hoarder. The case manager reported there was no heat and the home was not a place Mary could stay. My case manager also reported that the basement was flooded with water. Mary lived in a duplex and said the electric utility company had shut off the vacant side due to a safety issue. The water in the pipes on the vacant side had frozen and burst which had also flooded Mary's side. My case manager needed direction on what to do next. I told her to look around, collect any utility bills, bank statements, and any personal contacts she could find and bring Mary back to the office.

As Mary entered our office, I asked her if she was hungry. She was very hungry so we ordered some food for her, got her warmed up, and started to look at her documents to evaluate her situation. We called Adult Protective Services to see if they had her on file. They could not find her name. Next, we called the utility company to find out why her services had been shut off. The story Mary told us aligned correctly. I then asked Mary to come into my office and asked if she had any family I could call. She stated she had a daughter in another nearby state and another she didn't speak with who lived close by. Mary refused to give me their information so I further poked around for bits and pieces to hopefully find more information. I went to Facebook and entered her daughter's name and asked Mary if the lady I found on Facebook was her daughter. It was the right person so I messaged her to call my office as there was an emergency with her mother. Next, I needed to find the other daughter. Mary was very resistant to providing information but she stated that her daughter and son-in-law owned a store in a town nearby. We asked several questions of Mary about the second daughter to finally pin point the name of the business and contact information. We located and talked with her.

After getting the full story from the daughter's perspective, I asked Mary if we could set her up in a hotel until we could address the problems at her house. She agreed. Next, I needed to find out if Mary had any funds to pay for a hotel. She did not have a credit card and thought there wasn't any money in her bank account. With Mary's permission, we called the bank and found out Mary had much more money than she thought. We found a hotel that would allow her to stay on a cash basis due to circumstances. I brought Mary to her home and gathered paperwork and personal items for her hotel stay. I gave the hotel manager the information he needed and told him to call me if anything should happen.

The next day I spent hours on the phone gathering information. I called Adult Protective Services again and spoke with another individual. This person was helpful and said that this situation sounded familiar. She asked for Mary's address and found out the name they had on file did not match Mary's name. After talking with Mary about it, she disclosed her real name but stated she liked Mary better so had been using it as her name. Wow!

I spoke with her daughters and they were appreciative of our assistance. Mary had struggled with mental illness for a long time and the daughters refused to be immediately involved but offered to help at a distance. I attempted to put a plan together. We needed Mary's advance directives and found out she had a lockbox where all her paperwork was kept. We picked Mary up at the hotel and took her to the bank. We retrieved the items in the lock box and brought them back to my office. We had her paperwork but also an envelope with over $7,000 in cash. The next step was to make a plan to place Mary in an assisted living facility for respite until the family could make more permanent plans for her.

At the hotel, Mary made some poor judgments and hitched a ride to The Veteran's Home. We found this out when we went to pick up Mary and she wasn't at the hotel. She had told us several times that if she needs to leave her home, it is to be given to The Veteran's Home. Given that clue, we checked her home and then called The Veteran's Home. She was there and was safe.

Mary's home was not maintained previously due to her paranoia and mistrust of men. Mary struggled with this because she hated men and did not trust any of the utility workers or the electrician who were hired to fix her home. The situation spiraled out of control.

Mary's case manager at Adult Protective Services was also a male. She really hated him. When talking with him, he claimed he could not get Mary to give him any information. This puzzled me since when Mary was in my office we had a great conversation. I knew how to communicate with her, how to keep her calm and was able to gather information to help her.

Mary needed a medical appointment to assess her mental state and get her placed into a facility. Mary said she did not have a doctor. In my research, I discovered Mary had not seen her doctor in over 10 years. Mary got an appointment and was diagnosed with a type of dementia. We eventually got Mary placed into an assisted living facility for a respite stay and used her money from the safety deposit box to pay for her stay with the family's permission. Mary did not have any other assets so the family ended up taking over and had Mary permanently placed. Mary could not return home as it was declared unsafe.

What went wrong with Mary's situation? Her condition was sidelined. In talking with other healthcare professionals, many knew of Mary but no one stepped up to help her. The utility workers, the electrician hired to fix her home, the adult protective case manager, banking representatives, neighbors and family just ignored it. We hope this story opens your eyes to the potential dangers of not following up on a cognitive deficit and getting a proper diagnosis and treatment plan. As one human family, we need to gain knowledge on dementia and know the warning signs. We need to become educated on what to do when you come in contact with someone needing help. Mary's story will be one I will never forget.

Resources
There are so many options for resources so I am highlighting a few below:
- ➢ Alzheimer's' Association: www.alz.org
- ➢ Alzheimer's Foundation of America: www.alzfdn.org
- ➢ The Parkinson's Foundation: www.parkinson.org
- ➢ National Institute on Aging: www.nia.nih.gov/health/publication
- ➢ Teepa Snow, MS, OTR/L, FAOTA: www.teepasnow.com

Check with your local state resources such as Health and Human Services, or the Department of Aging.

Recommended Books
- ➢ "Learning to Speak Alzheimer's" by Joanne Koenig Coste

- ➢ "Creating Moments of Joy" by Jolene Brackey
- ➢ "Coach Broyles' Playbook for Alzheimer's Caregivers" by Frank Broyles
- ➢ "The Alzheimer's Family" by Robert B. Santulli, MD

Social Media Sites/Blogs
- ➢ Facebook – Closed group, "Memory People"
- ➢ Blog – "Alzheimer's Reading Room"

PART 2- MANAGING THEIR CARE

Chapter 10- Legal Stuff- Advanced Directives and Estate Planning
Patty Laychock

Estate planning and Advanced Directive planning are similar to buying life insurance. No one likes to think they are going to die but, truth is, we are all going to die at some point. Shouldn't we be sure if we are incapacitated due to an illness or accidents our wishes are met? Similarly, shouldn't your assets be divided the way you would like them to following your death? With no Advanced Planning, upon your inability to make decision or your death, many states have a default process for your advocate. This is usually a spouse, then adult children and so on. If you have no family members, the courts will assign you a guardian, maybe even someone you do not even know. Wouldn't you rather choose the person you felt was most capable?

The case of Nancy illustrates this dilemma. Nancy was in a persistent vegetative state after a serious automobile accident. She was dependent, lived in a long-term care facility and received tube feedings for many years.

On the basis of their belief that Nancy would not want to continue to live under these circumstances, her parents requested that the feeding tube be removed and that Nancy be allowed to die. The Missouri Supreme Court stated that no one could exercise Nancy's right to refuse treatment without "clear and convincing evidence" of her wishes. After a long and arduous struggle with the healthcare system and the courts, Nancy's family and attorney were able to present the sufficient evidence. The feeding was stopped and Nancy was allowed to die. *Cruzan v Commissioner,* Missouri Department of Health, 497 US 261 (1990).

What could have been done to prevent this long struggle with the courts and the healthcare system? Advanced Directives clarify your health care choices should you not be able to communicate yourself. You do not need a lawyer to prepare an Advance Directives; most states require 2 witnesses to the document. A person can change his or her advance directives at any time or even revoke the document completely. Always check with your State Health Department or Department of Aging as guidelines vary from state to state. Most state accept the **Five Wishes*** document. This document can be found at http://www.agingwithdignity.org. State-specific advance directives information and sample forms can be obtained at www.partnershipforcaring.org.

Types of Advanced Directives

Most states offer these documents Generally, they must be signed, witnessed and notarized by one or two adults.

> - **Living Will-** A Living Will is a legal document prepared in advance expressing your wishes for healthcare treatment should you become unable to do so. In this document you list exactly what type(s) of treatment you would want and those you would not want. The type(s) of treatment decisions you would be deciding on are: artificial life support, artificial nutrition, etc.

> - **Durable Power of Attorney or Medical Power of Attorney (POA)-** Also a legal document that differs from a Living Will in that you actually appoint a substitute decision maker. This is someone you have discussed your wishes to and can act as your advocate, if you are not able to communicate yourself. Your Medical Power of Attorney would be able to access your medical records, and discuss treatments with the medical community. The power of attorney is only active when you are unable to communicate your choices.

> - **Durable Power of Attorney for Finances-** This legal document allows you to appoint someone to assist with your finances and legal issues now and will act on your behalf should you become incapacitated; that is why this document is described as "durable". This appointment ends at your death.

If you do not have a Living Will or Medical Power of Attorney the courts will appoint a guardian to assist with your medical and financial decisions if you are incapacitated. This guardian may be someone you know or maybe an approved outsider appointed by the courts.

> - **CPR Directive or Out of Hospital Do Not Resuscitate Order-** (This is a totally different document then the "advanced directive"). In an emergency situation when 911 is called, Emergency medical personnel must legally attempt to resuscitate you, unless you have

a special "out-of-hospital- Do Not Resuscitate Order". Again check with your state because laws vary as most states only address situations of cardiac or respiratory arrest. In general, you and your doctor must sign a special form to prevent artificial resuscitation. You would wear a special identification bracelet or necklace so, in the event you were found unresponsive, you would not be resuscitated.

Estate Planning

- ➤ **Wills and Living Trusts-** In reference to the story about Nancy, who suffered a serious injury and later death, what happens to her assets? Without an estate plan, your assets will be distributed according to the probate laws in your state. The laws vary from state to state, so always be sure to get adequate legal advice. Some states will divide an estate equally between spouse and children. Therefore, your spouse may only get a fraction of your estate. Estate planning is not just for the wealthy. If you have any assets for example a home, a car, checking account, etc. You should be the one who decides who gets your assets, not the courts.

- ➤ **Last Will-** A will is a legal document where you chose who will receive your assets and you name one or two people to manage your estate upon your death. This is usually made public upon your death and will go through probate. Probate is when the courts review your will and then follow your wishes, unless someone contests it. Probate can be very expensive.

- ➤ **Living Trust-** A living trust is more common today than in the past. It allows you to control your assets during your life and then changes ownership to the named trustee upon your death. This document is not made public and does not go through probate. Therefore, your personal matters are not made public and your estate does not have to pay for probate.

The American Bar Association commission of law and aging states over 2/3 of the adult population have no Living Will or other advance directive. Without these directives you may lose your right to decide how you want to be treated should you become incapacitated or who acquires your assets upon your death. Advanced Directives are important for anyone over the age of 18. Estate planning is not just for the wealthy, it is for anyone with any assets at all: a savings account, a home, etc. Whenever starting your plan, check with your state health department or department on aging for state specific laws.

REMEMBER THESE IMPORTANT FACTS!
Advanced Directives
Living Will – you document your specific healthcare choices in case you become incapacitated.

Durable Power of Attorney- POA- You chose a specific person to make medical decisions for you, if you become incapacitate and cannot communicate

Financial Durable Power of Attorney – You chose someone to assist with your finances now and should you become incapacitate they will act on your behalf.

Estate Planning
Last Will - a legal document, you chose who will receive your assets and appoint someone to manage your estate upon your death. This document will be made public upon your death and will have to go through usually costly probate.

Living Trust – a legal document where your assets change ownership upon your death. This is not made public and does not go through probate.

Information for the American Bar Association Commission on Law and Aging states: Over 2/3 of the adult population have no Living Will or other advance directive.
 American Bar Association
Commission on Law and Aging
740 Fifteenth Street, NW, Washington, DC 20005
Phone: 202-662-8690
Internet: www.abanet.org/aging

Five Wishes
http://www.agingwithdignity.org

Chapter 11- Medical Equipment & Home Remodel
Eddie Morris

The Center for Disease Control defines "Aging in Place" as "the ability to live in one's own home and community safely, independently, and comfortably, regardless of age, income, or ability level."

Did You Know?
According to a recent report submitted by the Consumer Product Safety Commission, 370 Americans are injured every day in the bathtub or shower. One third of those injuries are serious enough to require a hospital visit. The majority of bathroom injuries are from seniors trying to stabilize themselves on shower doors, towel racks and other fixtures that were not designed for this purpose. A 2006 study by the American Association of Retired Persons found that 89 percent of respondents wanted to stay in their own homes as long as possible. This chapter includes suggestions for creating a safe environment. Becoming aware of all the options available will help you age in place successfully.

As we age, our mobility and physical strength diminish and many features of our homes that were once functional become challenging. As you consider and live out your early choices for retirement, you can modify your home to better support your body's changing needs to enable aging-in-place. Home modifications can be as simple as changing water faucet handles from knobs to levers or as broad as the formation of an elder cottage or mother-in-law suite on the property.

Suggestions for Elder Safe Modifications

➢ Widen hallways to accommodate a power scooter or power chair;
➢ Install countertops with rounded edges;
➢ Put lever-style handles on all doors;
➢ Install safety rails in hallways;
➢ Consider how the furniture is arranged, and determine if it provides safe place to lean as you walk through your home. There are a number of things you can do to make your home aging-in-place friendly;
➢ Can you enter and exit your house with ease? If not, ramps or vertical lifts may be a worthwhile investment. Auto ramps and car lifts are also practical solutions for seniors who want to leave the house on a regular basis. If you travel outside the home, plan ahead. If you use a cane or walker, do not leave it behind.
➢ Is the bathroom safe? The majority of injuries and falls among home-bound seniors take place in the bathroom. Incorporating non-slip surfaces and barrier-free baths, showers and other safety bath equipment such as grab bars and shower chairs make the bathroom less of a danger.

An easy start to an aging in place friendly home is to make it obstacle-free so you can prevent falls. A good opener is to stay ahead of the hoarding curve by removing clutter throughout the home: closets, drawers, cabinets, tabletops and frequently used rooms. Then, clear walkways for smoother, safer travels (considering walking, walkers and power scooters); move/rearrange bulky furniture to make for safe places to lean and remove trip hazards like power cords and high-pile or loose rugs. Home improvements, modifications and repairs can help older adults maintain their independence and prevent accidents.

While it is possible for the non-professional to assess all of the modifications required to make a home both accessible and safe for the elderly, the use of a professional occupational therapist can be worth the additional effort and is sometimes paid for by Medicare. There are two major considerations. First, it is important to recognize that aging is a progression, modifications to accommodate needs today might not be sufficient for needs 2 years in the future. Being able to project how your needs will change is of critical importance if you hope to make lifelong modifications in a single project.

Second, knowledge of assistive technologies is critical. There are many devices on the market today and more importantly a flood of new options become available each year. For the most cost-effective modifications, you need to be aware of the full breadth of products on the market today but also the tools that will be available in the near future.

Paying for Aging in Place

Dorothy said it right in the Wizard of Oz: "There's no place like home." You deserve dignity and peace as you age and to be able to stay in your own home for as long as possible. To understand the options available to pay for home modifications, it is helpful to understand some common terminology.

- ➤ Assistive Technology, Adaptive Technology (AT), refers to any tools or devices that enable independence for persons with disabilities.
- ➤ Environmental Accessibility Adaptations and Environmental Modifications are commonly used Medicaid phrases which simply mean home modifications.
- ➤ ECHO Units is an acronym for Elder Cottage Housing Opportunities. These are small, livable cottages designed specifically for seniors that can be placed temporarily on the property to allow an elderly person to live near but in their family's home. They are also referred to as Accessory Units, Mother-In-Law suites, Tiny Homes, detached bedrooms or less formally as Granny Flats. Your city housing codes will determine the extent of the structure that can be added.
- ➤ Universal Design is a phrase that means a product or building was designed with the needs of both the disabled and people without disabilities in mind.

In many cases, the financial burden of necessary modifications to your home and in-home care may seem overwhelming. Luckily, there are options available that will allow you to pay for the modifications and the care you need.

Medicare

If you are currently on Medicare, you need to look into the most recent long-term care options available on your plan. In certain scenarios, Medicare will pay for in-home care, including home health care, where someone will help you with personal care tasks when you are unable to accomplish those tasks for yourself.

It is important to note that Medicare is only a short-term solution for long-term care, such as when an individual fell and broke their hip and has been discharged from the hospital but still needs care. For a long-term care solution such as dementia care, etc., the answer would generally be Medicaid, not Medicare.

Medicaid's (HCBS) Waiver program

Medicaid's Home and Community Based Services (HCBS) Waiver program is designed to pay for many of the services that may be very difficult for you to afford on your own. Through this program, you are eligible for homemaking, personal care and even adult day health care services.

Veteran's Assistance

If you or your spouse is a veteran, you are eligible for a number of services through your veteran's benefits programs. Contact your local Veteran's Administration for more information about what services are available in your area. They can include everything from homemaker/home health care services to adult day care and hospice options. Veteran's assistance programs provide more individual discretion about how funds are used than many government programs, making them an ideal choice for many aging seniors.

Non-Medicaid Government Assistance

There are many states that offer assistance programs that will help you make modifications to your home or pay for long-term care. While not all states offer these programs, they are available in many states.

Private Health Insurance

Many private insurance companies offer options that will help pay for in-home care. They will also often cover durable medical equipment. With a doctor's order, this may include some of the equipment you need in order to be able to live safely in your home. Consult your insurance policy to see what benefits your insurance company offers. Not clear on the details? Call your insurance company and ask about their policies outright. In many cases, they'll be able to help you manage the maze of information provided in your policy to determine what benefits are available for you.

Long-Term Care Insurance

Do you own a Long-Term Care (LTC) insurance policy? This type of insurance policy can help you pay for a variety of LTC options including home care, assisted living care or a nursing home stay, as well as pay expenses for adult day care, care coordination and other services. You should be familiar with what is offered by your insurance policy.

Outside existing government programs and Insurance policies, it is helpful to differentiate between the other types of help that is available.

> - Some organizations, mainly governmental, offer low interest loans for home modifications or guarantee loans so that banks are less restrictive with their lending requirements. These loans, of course, need to be paid back.

> - Home improvement grants, on the other hand, are typically one-time and available for a specific home modification purpose and do not need to be re-paid.

> - Some organizations make free, long term loans of home modification equipment to the elderly. For example, they may

lend a senior a removable wheelchair that does not need to be returned until the senior moves from the home and no longer requires use of the ramp.

➢ Finally, to limit one's view of assistance to only financial assistance is to discount one's best option, which is to find free labor. Many organizations provide free labor to assist in home modifications. One well-known program which offers assistance to many individuals is Rebuilding Together. On a local level, one should consider contacting churches, high schools, fraternities, unions, independent living centers, Rotary, Lions and other clubs and neighborhood associations. Even if these institutions do not have an established volunteer home modification program, many will take on the project on a one-off basis.

"PayingForSeniorCare.com" maintains a searchable database of financial assistance programs (www.payingforseniorcare.com) of financial assistance programs that can help with the cost of home modifications. They have also authored articles specifically about paying for motorized wheelchairs and paying for bathroom safety modifications.

Consider visiting www.ageinplace.org for an ongoing update of options available that could help you on your journey to age in place successfully.

Chapter 12- How to Pay for Home Care
Bob Melcher

John and Betty knew each other from their days raising their respective families. But, by the time they were in their mid-fifties, John was a widower and Betty was a widow with a survivor's pension from her husband. John only had his income until he retired, then his social security and savings. They decided to marry, but found that Betty would lose her pension if they did, so they simply shared her home.

Forty years later as each approached their '90s John became ill with a degenerative disease and as his health failed, he required more and more help. They hired our home care agency to provide care, and John's illness lasted many years. Betty was also in poor health and while she should have had some light assistance, she did not.

John's savings were quickly depleted, so Betty took a reverse mortgage on her home to continue care. Those funds were adequate until John passed away but then Betty's needs increased and she had to hire more and more care. It was more expensive than her pension; in a weak real estate market there was no longer any equity in her home and because of her income, she did not qualify for public assistance. She even hired an "Elder lawyer" who was unable to find a way to pay or qualify for public aid. At this point, it seemed that Betty's only option was to enter a nursing home, have them take her pension and the remains of her home and let the State government pay for the rest. Luckily, one of John's sons was very successful and pitched in to pay half of Betty's bill.

The lawyer told Betty she should not have taken the reverse mortgage for John's care; John did qualify for assistance and since they had never married, it would not have affected Betty's assets. Betty would have been in the position that the State's regulations expected and would have been able to afford her own care. While Betty was no longer well off, she was able to stay in her home, but it could easily have gone the other way.

The moral of this story is that if you want control in your last years, you should get professional advice sooner rather than later. Today may not be too late.

Caring for a Senior can be very expensive but luckily, most seniors have assets that can be used for care and, unlike John and Betty, only very few must pay for care over an extended period. Other chapters of this book deal with choosing care, managing care, protecting your senior while they receive care and making sure that your senior has as good a quality of life as they can manage.

What the Government Pays for through Medicare and Medicaid
The Federal Government in the United States has two medical programs that apply to seniors; Medicare and Medicaid.

Medicare pays for medical care for people 65 and older (as well as for disabled people under 65). Medicare covers a variety of services, but only covers medically necessary home care. Typically, you would receive a few hours twice per week for bathing after surgery, but it can include much more as needed or much less. This help will be ordered by a Registered Nurse, who will visit you the first day you are home from the hospital. This nurse will also order physical therapy, occupational therapy and home medical treatments. I always tell people to accept whatever help Medicare provides; you already paid for it.

Medicaid or Title 19 pays for medical care for people who are financially unable to provide care for themselves. Medicaid is largely paid by the federal government but is administered by each state. When you hear about states that have rejected the affordable care act it is because they have rejected Medicaid changes, which will become expensive for the state in future years. Medicaid pays for home care under stringent conditions, with different rules in every state. Medicaid also pays for Nursing Home care, but not for independent or assisted living facilities. If you need Medicaid, you will need to go through a social worker for your town, county or state, each of which generally have social service support specifically for seniors.

Medicare and Medicaid do not pay for independent or assisted living and in many states will not pay for the kind of home care Visiting Angels provides. If the care is necessary, you will need to use a social worker or an elder attorney to determine exactly what they will pay for.

The complexity you face with Medicaid is that most people start with enough funds to pay for care that Medicaid will NOT take over when the funds run out. Private nursing homes in Connecticut, for example, charge between $9,100 and $16,425 per month, but when a client's funds run out they are required to accept Medicaid's much lower rate (just over $6,000 per month). Most nursing homes try very hard to have a high percentage of private paying clients simply because running a nursing home is expensive and private cases pay more. So the nursing homes accept patients who can afford 8-14 months of private pay services and take their required Medicaid residents from those who survive long enough to run out of money.

If you move into an assisted living facility and then run out of money, you will be evicted from the facility. If you cannot go home you will need to go into a nursing home, but may not have many options. Medicaid will pay, but you will probably have no choice in where you end up.

You have to think long and hard about your long term care plans:
> Be prepared by finding a nursing home you like. Choose one where you know patients and they like living there. Make sure it is Medicare certified.
> Find out how much that home would cost and how many months of private-pay they would demand.
> See an attorney who specializes in Elder Law for your state and figure out at what financial point you must decide about your future residence. The sooner you do this the better because you may want to buy specialized insurance to make sure you can pay for the facility you want or stay at home without the risk of ending up in a Medicaid-only institution.

What You Have to Pay for and What It Costs

If the time comes that you need assistance with your activities of daily living you will have a number of choices:

1) Live at home with assistance from friends, family or an agency like Visiting Angels.

2) Move to an independent living facility for which you will pay privately. This is a senior community where meals are prepared for you to be eaten in a dining room with other residents. These are generally very nice, very social places and often are specialized resorts. My parents spent their last decade at Tide Pointe on Hilton Head Island, South Carolina and they found it very rewarding. If you need additional care, like help bathing or dressing, you will pay an additional fee to an agency like Visiting Angels to provide that help.

3) Move to an Assisted Living facility, for which you would pay privately. Residents here receive limited help bathing, dressing, eating and with other activities, but if you need extended help, you would get that from an outside agency like Visiting Angels.

Since Government programs are your final (and for some people their only) option, you need to be aware of both state and federal regulations in order to keep that option open. For that, there are two pieces of advice:

1) Do not give away your assets. That is a job for your executor after you are gone. If you distribute your estate before you need care, you may not qualify for government programs if you distributed assets that might have paid for it.

2) Keep enough hard cash on hand to attract the right nursing home. I've heard anywhere from $40,000 to $180,000, but you should spend some time figuring out this option and knowing what sized payment will get you in your preferred location.

How to Pay for Care

After you have checked with your attorney and the local social workers (every state has different programs and you might just get lucky) then here are the main ways people pay for their home care:

Veteran's Administration Aide and Attendance

This program has the most convoluted application process I know of. At a time when the Veteran who can use these services is in great distress and has a towering need for help, they are subjected to a dismal application process and made to wait at least four months, sometimes years, for the help that is due them.

We worked with three Veterans whose families applied for them and none ever collected a penny. All three Veterans died before their applications were accepted and the application delay stole the benefit they had earned from them. If you or your spouse:

1) Served in the military for at least 90 days,
2) Honorably discharged,
3) Served at least one day during defined periods of war,
4) Need assistance with two or more activities of daily living, or have specific debilitating medical conditions
5) Have less than $19,000 per year in income after you have deducted medical expenses
6) Less than $80,000 (excluding one car and one home) in assets (This amount is based on a sliding scale w/ age. A senior in their 70's the amount of assets is $60K, when a senior is in their 80-84 the amount is 40K, from 85-89 the amount is $30K, any senior over the age of 90, under 20K)

You may qualify for up to $2,120 (2015) per month in Aide and Attendance Pension benefits. You get these by applying for a veteran's pension and specifying what benefits you want. It is a very difficult application and I've never heard of anyone applying by themselves and getting approved.

The good news is that there are licensed organizations who will apply for this benefit for you and pay for your care while waiting for the Veteran's Administration to approve and pay the claim. We refer all qualifying Veterans to such an agency.

After three Veterans died before their self-applications were accepted, we decided to direct all our qualifying clients to a specialized agency, which is a fast and easy alternative. We, as Americans, should do a better job for our Veterans.

Long-Term-Care Insurance

Long Term Care insurance is a specialized product which pays for care under certain circumstances. Some policies allow that care to be at home and all allow the care to be given in residency in a Nursing Home.

These policies are very expensive, so the people who buy them generally have assets to protect or a strong desire to be sure care will be there when they need it.

Generally, the policy holder qualifies for benefits if:
1) They have been diagnosed with dementia and require supervision as a result;
2) They require help with three or more activities of daily living (activities like bathing, preparing meals, laundry, shopping, errands, dressing, toileting, ambulation or driving).

Types and Limits
Some insurance will only pay for a Medicare approved facility, but even if your policy specifies a facility, times have changed, so you should ask if they will pay for in-home care. People buy this insurance to protect assets. Long Term Care insurance (LTC) is expensive and policies generally have a limit for each day and a number of days before you are eligible for payments. Some also have a total policy limit. You will need a professional to help you buy this insurance and you will need to be very realistic. It can be very expensive.

Here is a typical policy that is 30 years old:
1) Pays up to $171.00 per day;
2) The insured pays for the first 90 days, but must have their claim approved and file invoices for those 90 days;
3) Has a lifetime limit of $167,580 dollars (140 weeks)

There are new policies that you can buy even after you are diagnosed. These policies pool the risk for people in similar situations and you pay for the average length of care, thus removing any risk of running out of money because you lived longer than average (half do just that).

Savings
If you have savings, you will be prevented from giving them away so that you qualify for care from the government. Instead, you will need to use your savings to pay for care, but then the state will take over when your funds run out. Work with a specialized attorney; it is critical that you get this right.

Reverse Mortgage

A reverse mortgage is when you give up equity in your home for cash. It is like selling it with lifetime rights to reside in the home. Reverse mortgages are heavily regulated, so, while in the past there were some abusive programs, now you can be very sure you will have use of your home as long as you wish.

Cash Value in Life Insurance

If you no longer need your life insurance, there are companies that will buy your paid-up policy and pay you a discounted rate for the benefits. An example would be if your spouse had passed away but your whole life policy was up to date.

Family

Often a care recipient's family will chip in and pay for some or all of this kind of care. As you have read, financing your own or a loved one's care can be expensive and complicated. When we look at the alternatives, they are even more complicated and more expensive:

Situation	Cost of In-Home	Alternative
Mildly Unsteady / History of falls	3 hours daily at home for basic fall prevention activities $2,000 per month	Hospitalization as a result of a fall, changed life, need for $6,000 -$18,000 per month in care
Mild Dementia / help with basic chores	3 hours 3 times a week $850 per month	Memory Care Community $5,000 per month (average)
Advanced Dementia	24/7 care and supervision, $6,000 to $11,000 per month	Memory Care or Nursing Home $6,000 to $18,000 per month
Bedbound	24/7 care $6,000 to $11,000 per month	Nursing Home $6,000 to $18,000 per month

It is important to know that staying at home often comes with the cost of owning and maintaining the house, but in every instance, it is probably going to be less expensive to stay at home, and the care recipient is going to be happier in his or her familiar environment.

While this may be too complicated for now, when you do need care, just call your local Visiting Angels office and we can you how much it will cost to have care at home. If there is any confusion about how to pay for it, we can refer you to either an elder attorney who will help you organize your affairs so that you maintain control or to whichever service provider is listed above.

Chapter 13- The Art of Helping Aging Parents Manage Their Finances
Page Cole

Every Case Is Unique.

Anna and Dave just celebrated their 50th wedding anniversary last month. Their kids were thrilled that everyone was able to come together for this milestone in their parents' lives. In the days leading up to the event, their daughter Cheryl had taken the lead for making most of the arrangements. Her parents were insistent that they were the ones throwing this party for each other, so they were paying for everything. Her father added Cheryl to his checking account and for the first time ever, Cheryl had access to a large portion of her parents' financial information. What she found was shocking.

Cheryl discovered that her parents had been regularly overdrawn multiple times in the past, and that there were a number of unusual purchases and monthly drafts to their account. An initial round of gentle but probing questions were met with embarrassment and defensiveness. Cheryl decided to wait until after the big celebration to push for more information, but she knew something had to be done.

Families like this one, and maybe just like yours should realize that this is a very common situation. In a recent study by researchers at the Federal Reserve, Harvard, New York University and the University of Singapore, they found that financial decision-making abilities peak around 53 years old, but that it begins to diminish from there. About half of adults between 80 and 89 years of age suffer from dementia or have a diagnosis of cognitive impairment without dementia, the study noted. (Social Science Research Network)

So how can adult children who are concerned about their parents' finances help? What can they do and how can they intervene in a way that is productive to the financial situation without damaging the relationships of everyone involved?

Beginning The Process
Reasons You Made Need to Help
There are a variety of reasons why a parent or parents may have moved to the point where they need some assistance with their finances. Among those reasons are:

- One or both may have developed mental impairments like Alzheimer's or other types of dementia;
- One or both may have physical impairments (like arthritis or diminished sight) that either severely limit or prevent the ability to write checks or sign documents;
- Family may have sensed or seen an increased vulnerability to scammers;
- A surviving spouse may be facing the loss of a spouse who handled all of the couple's finances to that point;
- In a transient world, immigrant parents might lack English skills or familiarity with banking and tax procedures;

> There may simply be a lack of financial assets, due to poor retirement planning, a downturn in the economic market or bad financial choices by the aging parent.

Any of these reasons might be sufficient enough for an adult child to begin the process of offering assistance. Sadly, many seniors find themselves facing more than one of these scenarios. So what should be done next?

Having "The Talk" With Your Parents

It is important that you initiate this conversation earlier than later. Maybe you do not think your parents have any need for you to help manage their finances. Then NOW is the perfect time for you to initiate the discussion! Here are some suggestions for you to consider as you look towards initiating this discussion regarding their finances.

First, consider using current events as a starter to the conversation. For instance, you might say, "With all of the turmoil in the economy and stock market, I'm curious… how have you guys made decisions regarding investing for your retirement?"

Another approach might be to ask them to start the conversation. Simply approach the subject by saying, "What would you tell us about financial planning? We want to know that we've got our bases covered as we retire someday, so tell me what things you would suggest?" Talk about your own financial situation & financial planner, and see if they have any similar stories about finances. By talking to them about what they did in the past, you may be able to easily transition the discussion to the here and now.

If you sense hesitancy or resistance to this discussion, consider using "love for family" as a motivation for the discussion. That emphasis can be about your care and concern for them, as well as your understanding of their love for you and your extended family members over the years.

As you progress deeper into this conversation, it is critical that you use caution in how far or how hard you push this conversation. It is understandable that you want to help, but your parents are entitled to their privacy in many respects. Some issues are not your business, or the timing may not be right for you to push this conversation very hard.

Try to stay as positive with your parents as you can. Make sure they understand your goal is to help them stay on the financial road they have built. It helps them accept assistance while still allowing them to maintain their personal dignity and pride.

Finally, get other family members involved as best suits your situation. If you understand the dynamics of your family and there are other family members that your parents might be more responsive to, then visit with those individuals earlier to see if you can enlist their help, or gain some insight from them in how to constructively handle this situation.

Assess The Situation
It is critical that before you make any decisions or take any actions that you make a clear assessment of their current situation. There are so many factors that could impact the situation it is important you conduct a thorough study of the situations around their unique financial, health & personal

situations. Consider these issues and use it as your checklist as you prepare to talk with your parents.

➢ Take the time to visit with your parents' friends, medical professionals and other extended family members. Discover what their opinion is regarding the mental capacity of your loved ones. Look for input that might point toward increasing forgetfulness or other signs of confusion.

➢ Perform a personal walk through inspection of your parents' house. Signs that could be red flags include bills scattered around, piles of unopened mail or paper or multiple sweepstakes and contest mailings. The absence of an organized filing system or a way for them to manage their money could be another sign they might need help managing their finances.

➢ Sort through their bank statements, checkbook, credit statements and any other charge accounts. As you do, look for instances of double payments, unusual transactions and withdrawals and checks made out to unknown or questionable entities. Also note whether they might have failed to record deposits or list in the check register any checks they have written.

➢ Go over any substantial or unusual transactions with your parents to discern whether or not there may be a problem. Many times the explanation or lack of explanation may spread some light on the situation, and help you to further understand the existence or the depth of a problem.

➢ As you are auditing their monthly expenditures, see if the payments for things like utilities, rent, mortgage or insurance payments were made consistently and accurately.

➢ As you sort through their mail, do you see collections letters, bills with late fees, multiple bills unopened or uncashed checks? Make sure that you are able to locate used check registers, statements from financial accounts and other important financial information that they should have been able to readily access and organize.

➤ Does the elder seem confused or forgetful when discussing the specifics of their finances with you? Do they truly seem to have a clear and thorough knowledge of their financial accounts?

➤ Look for clues as to whether your loved one has spent large sums on home shopping network or internet purchases, as well as lotteries or contests. You should also look for unusually large donations or multiple donations to charities or non-profits.

➤ Look for signs that your parents may have been the victims of fraud or financial crimes, including investment fraud, predatory lending, or telemarketing scams.

The Money Big Picture
To best help discern whether or not your parents need help with their finances and to what extent they may need that help, it is beneficial if you can get a "big picture" or and "aerial view" of their financial picture. These are some of the major issues you will want to understand as you proceed.

1) Do they have a financial planner? If the answer is no, then they are more likely to need some help with their overall financial situation. However, if they do have a financial planner then some of the larger issues such as investments or balance of retirement portfolio, ease of access to funds and other issues may already have safeguards built in.
2) A major part of your parents' financial picture has to do with their insurance issues. Do they have Supplementary Healthcare Insurance to cover medical costs not covered by Medicare? Have they planned ahead for long term care issues by purchasing long term care insurance?
3) Find out whether a will is in place, whether trusts have been established or other long term financial management plans have

been set up. It will be important to know who helped set these up, and who currently has access or control of them.

4) Establish a Durable Power of Attorney or other financial legal statuses. You will also want a clear understanding of any property they own, as well as other investments. Having a clear understanding of their current financial situation is a prerequisite to determining whether or not your assistance is needed in managing those finances.

5) Finally, there may be some situations where you may need to explore what your legal options are regarding the management of their finances. Although you should only seek a legal remedy to involving yourself in the management of their finances as a last resort, that does not mean you wait until that point to discover what your options are in that arena.

Plan The Work, Work The Plan

As you begin the process of helping your parents with their finances, be vigilante to watch for danger signs regarding their ability to manage their finances, or trouble that they may be experiencing in handling their finances. Watching for danger signs like piles of unopened mail or unpaid bills, overdrafts or mistakes in their bank accounts or a general sense of confusion in conversations regarding their finances.

Start small as you move forward with your plan. Your parents may be thrilled to have your help, but it is more likely that there will be at least a small amount of caution and even some negative feelings about your involvement in their finances. You might make a master list of the various areas where you could be of assistance to your parents with their finances and list them in order of "most important" to "it can wait". Better to help successfully in one area where your involvement is critical than to cause anger and resentment by pushing too hard, too fast.

Open the lines of communication with your parents by remembering they need your respect and to retain their own dignity as bad as they need your help balancing their checkbook. Your conversations about finances will be received better if they sense patience rather than control, and conversation rather than dictating to them what will happen. Communicate consistently with them regarding your involvement. They may appreciate a weekly conversation over coffee or a detailed email from with bullet points and copies of statements. Whatever works best in your situation, make it happen, and be consistent.

If you are helping them manage their retirement funds, it is critical that you choose safe, modest investments over risky ones. Younger adults have the luxury of making investments that have a greater level of risk because they have more time for potential losses to make up with future gains. It is important that in managing the money that represents the majority of their retirement income that you not handle those funds flippantly or in a risky manner.

One of the most important parts of your plan is to effectively organize the important financial documents they have. That includes bank statements, retirement fund statements, stock and investment documents. It is also important to gather any insurance policies, deeds or titles to property of all kinds and even items like jewelry, coins or other valuables.

If you are going to be assisting them in all respects of their finances, that will also include gathering and organizing all of their estate planning documents, like a will, living will, trust or power of attorney paper work. It is critical that you not only know where this information is, but that you understand its value, and you are able to lay your hands on it easily and quickly if needed.

Now that you have gathered all of their financial information together, you may need to assess and determine the best banking practice for your situation. Will you set up a joint account where the assets in the account actually belong to both you and the parent? Or will you simply have a single owner account where you are added as an authorized signer. Sit down and talk with a banker and a financial advisor to determine which of these is best for you.

Now you've reached a point at which you are ready to build a financial status inventory. First, define what the total monthly income is of your parents. Document where it comes from and how often it comes in. Next, determine what their total monthly expenses are. Discover any important deadlines for payments or financial commitments. One excellent tool for helping them manage their finances is gaining access to their various financial accounts online. If you have online access, you can manage and move assets, pay bills and even set up recurring online payments of various bills.

Financial Assistance Quiz

So how can you tell if your parents genuinely need assistance with their finances? We've mentioned looking for various red flags, opening communication with them about their finances and investigating their finances as you are able to. The following quiz is a good tool to use as you determine whether the time has come for you to begin helping your parents with their money.

Ask these questions about them and their situations:

1) Does your parent have trouble physically writing checks?
2) Does your parent regularly have piles of unpaid bills around their home?
3) Have you noticed excessive mail from charitable organizations?
4) Do your parents get defensive or protective when discussions of their finances come up?
5) Does your parent seem to be making unusual or excessive purchases?
6) Has your parent complained about jewelry, cash or other valuables missing?
7) Does your parent have a debilitating physical or mental condition that would hinder effective management of their own finances?
8) Have you seen incorrect or duplicate payments by your parents?
9) Have you noticed a larger than normal credit card debt, or new credit accounts?

The bottom line is there is more than one bottom line. Of course the finances of your parents are critically important. They need the assets they possess to live, enjoy life and care for their needs. But beyond that, they need your respect and to retain their dignity in the process. You can make that happen!

Chapter 14- When It Is Time to Take Away the Keys
Paul Gach

There are times in the life of many families where they are faced with the challenges of an elderly loved one whose driving skills have diminished to the point of serious concern. The family may be wrestling with questions like:

- When is the right time to take away the keys from an elderly parent?
- How do you identify the signs that intervention is required?
- How do you approach the conversation with the person?
- What is next if the person refuses to relinquish their keys after your conversation?
- Who else might be able to influence them to stop driving? If necessary, you can request your state Department of Motor Vehicles to evaluate a driver.
- What transportation alternatives might be available in your area?

This is no small matter; it is a critical issue of protecting your family member and one of public safety. It is not often but occasionally accidents involving senior drivers end up making National News and plastered all over the networks and the internet. One of the most serious accidents occurred back in 2003 and the headlines read:

Car Plows Through Crowd in Santa Monica, Killing 9

The 86-year-old driver apparently loses control and speeds 2 1/2 blocks through a farmers' market. More than 50 are hurt, 15 critically. **July 17, 2003**|*Joel Rubin, Daren Briscoe and Mitchell Landsberg | Times Staff Writers*

An 86-year-old man drove his car the length of the Santa Monica Farmers' Market early Wednesday afternoon, apparently reaching freeway speeds as he plowed through a crowd of terrified summer shoppers, killing at least nine people, including a 3-year-old girl.
More than 50 people were hospitalized, 15 of them with critical injuries, after the driver of Santa Monica sped for 2 1/2 blocks through a market renowned as one of the region's culinary treasures.

Police said it appeared that the driver had lost control of his car.
"His statement is, he possibly hit the gas instead of the brake," said Santa Monica Police "He said he tried to brake and he couldn't stop the vehicle."

Tests conducted immediately afterward showed that the driver was not under the influence of drugs or alcohol. Investigators said they did not believe he had any medical problem that might have caused the crash.

Several of the witnesses ran after the car trying to get the license plate. Farmers were yelling, 'Get that guy! Get that guy!' But when they got there, it was just this old man sitting there in his car with an air bag blown up in his face, looking like he didn't know where he was." The crowd pulled the driver out of the car and he looked like he was in some kind of numb state. He wasn't freaking out according to a witness.

The dead included six men, two women and a baby, officials said. Police said the driver had just left a nearby post office and was headed west on Arizona when he spotted the farmers market blocking his path. It was at that point that he apparently hit the gas instead of the brakes.

Daniel Vomhof, a San Diego area forensic consultant for traffic accidents, said such confusion between the brake and the accelerator can occur in drivers of all ages, although most commonly when they are behind the wheel of an unfamiliar car. He said the mistake typically compounds itself as a driver panics, stepping harder on the gas in the mistaken notion that the brakes have failed. "Things go from bad to worse instead of bad to better,"

The driver, a retired professional, had started his day uneventfully with him leaving his home to mail a letter to his great-niece. (How many times have you heard your loved one say, "I'm just going to the grocery store, or I'm just going out to eat?) This driver's ordeal ended up killing 10 people, injuring more than 70 and being convicted of 10 counts of vehicular manslaughter with gross negligence.

Anne McCartt, senior vice president for research at the Insurance Institute of Highway Safety (IIHS), says older drivers are often unfairly demonized. For one thing, they are less likely than other groups to speed and drive drunk. And no group of drivers is more hazardous than teenagers, with their combination of inexperience and recklessness. While teens mature and become safer, increasing maturity has the opposite effect on the old. Once people turn 70, their crash rates start to tick up. After 80, the acceleration is marked. Seniors over eighty years old have a higher collision rate per mile traveled of any age group except for teens, and their rate of fatal collisions per mile traveled is the highest of all drivers.

As older drivers decline physically or cognitively, many do loosen their grip on the wheel voluntarily. The IIHS reports that those 70 and over drive less than half as many miles annually as middle-aged drivers. Numerous studies show that many older people restrict their time on the road by no longer driving at night, avoiding freeways, or staying home during bad weather.

That's the ideal—self-recognition and the support of loving family leading the older person to accept it is the end of the road. Many elderly people do not accept this needed change willingly. When rational discussion fails, some people suggest disabling the car, filing down the keys, and canceling the vehicle registration. Even then, after a lifetime of being law-abiding, elderly motorists may go rogue; drivers may continue to drive without a driver's license, car registration, or insurance coverage. Never cancel the insurance if there remains a chance they will drive. In fact, if they are still unwilling to stop driving consider getting an umbrella insurance policy should the worse occur.

From my experience, families would rather talk about funeral plans with their parents than talk about taking away the car keys. Although discussions to determine our loved ones' lasts wishes are difficult and uncomfortable at best, we all know it is inevitable and we do not decide when our demise will occur. On the other hand, revoking someone's privilege to drive is considered an optional choice. It is even more challenging when you consider typical family dynamics have changed, as the role of the adult child shifts and they become the "parent" in the family. In our parents' eyes we are still wet behind the ears and do not know what is best for them. However, in many cases it is not really optional. Understanding the effect aging has on driving abilities, having the right approach and the right timing is going to make this conversation less arduous for everyone involved.

I do not want this chapter to be filled with statistics, however I feel compelled to provide some information about how factors contributing to accidents change as we age.

The following information is from the Insurance Institute for Highway Safety:

Top driver factors among older drivers, by driver age (percent)	Ages 70+	Ages 35-54
Inadequate surveillance[1]	33	22
Gap/speed misjudgment	6	3
Heart attack or other medical incapacitation	6	4
Failure to obey traffic controls or other illegal maneuver	6	4
Daydreaming	6	4

[1] Surveillance errors included looking but not seeing and failing to look.

About 66% of older driver inadequate surveillance errors and 77 % of their gap (distance misjudgment) were made when they turned left at intersections. On the lighter side of these numbers, in my opinion, it is highly probable that the 70+ group is hardly ever distracted by texting.

Conclusions from the IIHS

- ➢ Inadequate surveillance and gap/speed misjudgment errors more prevalent among older than middle-aged drivers, especially for older women. However, men are more than twice as likely to make illegal maneuvers and experience medical incapacitation.

- ➢ Efforts to reduce older driver crash involvements should focus on diminishing likelihood of the most common driver errors

- ➢ Focus on countermeasures that remove left turns across traffic or simplify them, such as:
  - o Protected left-turn signals (green arrows)
  - o Roundabouts
  - o Diverging diamond interchanges

- ➢ Vehicle-to-vehicle and vehicle-to-infrastructure communications, cross-traffic alert

Despite their growing numbers, older drivers are involved in fewer fatal collisions than in the past. Between the years of 1997 and 2013 fatal collisions were down 30% among 70+ drivers. Some newer vehicle features that help protect occupants of all ages are especially beneficial to older occupants. Side airbags with head and torso protection have been estimated to reduce fatalities in nearside impacts by 45 percent for front seat occupants ages 70 and older, which is significantly larger than the 30 percent reduction estimated for front seat occupants ages 13-49. The safety belts in older cars tended to be less effective for older occupants than for other occupants, but modern safety belts with pre-tensioners and load limiters are generally equally effective for adults of all ages. The same is true of frontal airbags. Front crash prevention systems, especially those with autonomous braking, are effective in reducing rear-end crashes. Another benefit to all drivers has been design changes in larger vehicles like trucks that reduce the damage caused when impacting smaller and lighter automobiles.

Today's elderly people are more fit than past generations, which also increased the probability of surviving a crash. However, fragility accounted for 77 percent of the higher death rates compared to middle-age drivers during a 2005-08 study.

Is It Time to Hang Up the Keys?

How would you react if you were sitting in the back seat, one of your parents were driving and they became slightly confused when it came time to take an exit? Alternatively, how would you react if they brushed a curb while driving down the road? Most people wouldn't consider either situation alarming, but what if your loved one got lost on the way to the grocery store or some other place they had been to dozens of times before? What if your mom said to you, "I had to do 85 miles per hour to stay in front of a tractor-trailer?"

There is no set age that a person becomes an unsafe driver. Many perfectly capable active 85+ year olds are safer drivers than many younger drivers. So do not just assume because of age a person is not a capable driver. In the past, there hasn't been any widely published "established criteria" to determine when a person should stop driving. However, it is easy to find information from some organizations like the Insurance Institute of Highway Safety and AARP that have lists of warning signs for unsafe driving many of which will be included below.

One must consider the drivers physical and cognitive capabilities and if diminished does it impair driving capabilities. Depending on the degree of impairment, driving may no longer be possible once a person's vision, hearing, physical mobility and/or reaction time have become impaired by old age, medications or diseases that robbed them of cognitive abilities such as memory, judgment and understanding.

Since driving abilities change over time observing personal and driving behaviors need to be done periodically. One instance of a negative driving experience may not be a reason to revoke their license, be sure to take notes to compare the frequency of occurrences. Some observations can be made in the home; however, it is important to ride with the person.

Anytime observations:

- ➤ Impaired hearing and refuses to wear hearing aids
- ➤ Impaired sight and refuses to wear glasses
- ➤ Impaired movement (difficulty moving head, hands or legs etc.)
- ➤ Problems understanding or following instructions
- ➤ Forgetfulness
- ➤ Falls asleep during conversations
- ➤ Impaired from new or changed medications (determine if temporary or permanent)
- ➤ Appears fearful or scared of driving or excessively tired after driving
- ➤ Uses a co-pilot
- ➤ Scrapes or dents on the car, mailbox or garage
- ➤ Listen for clues in stories about driving

Driving Observations:

- Fails to stop at stop signs or lights (take immediate action)
- Drives on the wrong side of the road or in the shoulder (take immediate action)
- Confused the gas and brake pedals (take immediate action)
- Stopped in traffic for no apparent reason (take immediate action)
- Delayed response to potential danger, on or near the road
- Gets lost more than usual, especially in familiar places
- Near misses/ Close calls
- Recent tickets for moving violations or accidents
- Makes abrupt lane changes, braking or acceleration
- Drifts into other lanes, or moving into wrong lane
- Has close calls or more fender benders than usual
- Fails to use turn signal or keeps signal on without changing lanes
- Troubles navigating turns, especially left-hand turns
- Drives at inappropriate speeds
- Easily distracted while driving
- Parking inappropriately
- Hitting curbs
- Riding the brake
- Troubles reading signs or navigating directions
- Fails to pay attention to signs, signals or pedestrians
- Misses exits or backs up after missing an exit
- Reacts slowly to changes in driving environment (turning on headlights & windshield wipers, slowing for snow and ice)
- Notices the irritation and honking of other drivers but doesn't seem to understand, or seems oblivious to the frustration of other drivers
- Decrease in confidence while driving
- Increased agitation or irritation when driving

Now you have information about your family member's physical and cognitive condition and their driving capabilities. Armed with this information you can correctly decide whether it is time to "have the talk" with them.

A driver's license signifies more than the ability to drive a car; it is a symbol of freedom and self-sufficiency, the ability to drive to restaurants, to stores and visit friends. In my father's case, he was more upset and depressed when he lost his driver's license than when he lost his right leg to diabetes. During your conversation, remember:

- **Be respectful.** Remember this is a major life-changing event that takes away part of their freedom to come and go as they please.

- **Give specific examples.** Do not sugar coat the situation by generalizing, use examples from your observations about their physical and cognitive conditions, and your observations of their driving.

- **Help find alternatives.** You can offer concrete help, such as researching transportation options or offering rides when possible. Other possibilities:
  - Local Area Agencies on Aging will be aware of transportation services
  - Ride Sharing- offer to share the transportation responsibilities and costs with family, friends and neighbors or return the favor by cooking meals or helping with other household activities.
  - American Red Cross, some will assist those who have no other means of transportation to and from critical medical appointments. Drivers will pick you up from your home, take you to your appointment and then return you home when your appointment is over.
  - Local Public Bus Service may offer transportation for disabled elderly aged 60+ at a minimal cost to medical appointments, dialysis, senior nutrition centers, paid employment and grocery shopping...
  - Local churches and nonprofit organizations may have a network of volunteers who offer flexible transportation for various purposes.

- Taxi service or depending on your location Uber or Lyft. In select cities, UberASSIST is designed to provide additional assistance to seniors and people with disabilities.

➤ **Understand the difficulty of the transition.** Do not dismiss their feelings but try to help with the transition as much as possible. If it is safe, try slowly transitioning them out of driving by limiting nighttime or interstate driving.

You may be blessed and they will agree to hand over their keys and license. Whether they freely give up their license or have them taken, exchange it for an identification card from the Department of Motor Vehicles (DMV) for identification purposes. However, do not be surprised if it takes several conversations if not an argument to convince them.

If this fails, the next step is to enlist the help of impartial professionals. I would recommend informing them of your observations at the meeting or before so they understand there is a valid concern. Older people are more inclined to take recommendations from their general physician or ophthalmologist so enlist them to discuss giving up the keys.

➤ **Find strength in numbers**. If more than one family member or close friend has noticed, it is less likely to be taken as nagging. They may also listen to an impartial party, such as a doctor or attorney.

If your attempts to obtain their keys and license are still unsuccessful then another avenue is to request a medical examination from your state Department of Motor Vehicles (DMV). States have various standards for licensing drivers however; their processes should be similar for evaluating driver capabilities. You can find your state's requirements on your state's DMV website as well as required forms. As an example, information for North Carolina is presented below.

Medical Evaluation Program in North Carolina

Medical Evaluation Program is responsible for gathering and evaluating the medical information of licensed drivers or applicants for driver licenses who are currently suffering from qualified disabilities that could have an impact on highway safety.

The Medical Evaluation Program's mission is to provide scientific and medical services to evaluate drivers who may suffer from conditions that adversely affect their ability to safely operate a motor vehicle. The Program's medical staff reviews medical records and statements from attending physicians in conjunction with driving records. Using their knowledge and experience in medicine and public health, they analyze this information and provide a recommendation as to what, if any, restrictions should be placed on a driver license. Their goal is to protect highway safety without causing unnecessary hardship on the driver.

Anyone can request that a driver be evaluated, if believed to be medically impaired, as long as the request is in writing and signed. Anonymous requests are not accepted. Reports of medical impairment are most often received by:

> - The driver license examiners ask a series of health related questions. If there is a concern about the driver, the examiner will conduct a road test and give the customer a medical report form to be completed by his physician. After completion, the form is returned to the Medical Evaluation Program.
> - Family members may ask for a re-examination of their parents, aunts, uncles, etc. DMV requires this request to be in writing and signed by the family member.
> - Physicians may send information to DMV about patients that they feel may be at risk to themselves or others.
> - DMV reviews all accident reports to determine whether a health problem could have contributed to the accident. If a health problem is suspected, the Medical Evaluation Program will send a letter and medical form to the driver.

- ➢ Law enforcement officers may send reports of drivers who they have observed with poor driving habits that could be related to a health problem (vision, slow reaction time, reports of blackouts, falling asleep).
- ➢ The court system may send involuntary commitments and incompetency orders to be entered into a driving record. There are many medical conditions that could affect one's ability to safely operate a motor vehicle. The following list gives some examples:
  - Seizures
  - Cardiovascular disorders (irregular rhythms, uncontrolled high blood pressure)
  - Respiratory disorders requiring oxygen
  - Diabetes with spells of unconsciousness
  - Impairment of limbs, back or neck (Cerebral Palsy, stroke, injury, etc.)
  - Cognitive impairment (stroke, head injury, dementia, etc.)
  - Vision impairment (cataracts or glaucoma)
  - Psychiatric disorder
  - Neurologic disorder (Parkinson's, dementia, other neurodegenerative disorders)
  - Substance abuse disorder
  - Sleep disorders (such as narcolepsy);

This doesn't mean that anyone with any of the above medical conditions should not drive. After reviewing a person's fitness to drive, the licensing agency may renew, remove, or restrict the license. These restrictions could be any one or several of the following:
- ➢ Corrective lenses
- ➢ Daylight driving only
- ➢ 45 MPH/No interstate driving
- ➢ To/From work, doctor, church, (anywhere within a safe distance of home)
- ➢ Within a radius of home
- ➢ With a licensed driver
- ➢ Other restrictions that safely allow a person to continue driving

These restrictions or the revoked status of a license can be temporary. Provided the reasons for the restrictions or revocation have improved or can be controlled by means of proper medication. Additional evaluations are dependent on the medical condition and whether it is progressive or stabilized. Evaluations can be as short as once every six months or as long as once every four years. The person evaluated can also file an appeal and will have to provide proof of their fitness to drive safely.

The very last option is to just take the keys or disable the car. This is not recommended at all because it can obviously cause conflict. In fact, there are documented cases of children having had the elder's car removed and then were under investigation by police when the elder person (even Mom or Dad) filed a stolen vehicle report. It is the hope that you can keep resolve driving issues without additional emotional strife.

For your reference is a table the Insurance Institute of Highway Safety has complied which provides the length of time for which licenses can be renewed, renewal methods and vision certification requirements for the general population and the older driver population.

State	License Renewal for General Population	License Renewal for Older Population	Proof of Adequate Vision for General Population	Proof of Adequate Vision for Older Population	Mail or Online renewal permitted for General Population	Mail or Online renewal permitted for Older Population
Alabama	4 years	4 years	no	no	no	no
Alaska	5 years	5 years	when renewing in person	69 and older, every renewal	both, every other renewal	not permitted 69 and older
Arizona	12 years	5 years for people 65 and older	every renewal	every renewal	no	no
Arkansas	8 years	8 years	every renewal	every renewal	no	no
California	5 years	5 years	when renewing in person	70 and older, every renewal	both, limited to 2 consecutive renewals	not permitted 70 and older

State	License Renewal for General Population	License Renewal for Older Population	Proof of Adequate Vision for General Population	Proof of Adequate Vision for Older Population	Mail or Online renewal permitted for General Population	Mail or Online renewal permitted for Older Population
Colorado	5 years	5 years	every renewal	every renewal	both, limited to 2 consecutive renewals online or every other renewal by mail	by mail, every other renewal for people 66 and older
Connecticut	6 years	2 years or 6 years for people 65 and older, personal option	no	no	no	no
Delaware	8 years	8 years	every renewal	every renewal	no	no
District of Columbia	8 years	8 years	every renewal	every renewal	both, every other renewal	not permitted 70 and older
Florida	8 years	6 years for people 80 and older	when renewing in person	80 and older, every renewal	both, every other renewal	both, every other renewal
Georgia	5 or 8 years, personal option	5 years for people 59 and older	every renewal	every renewal	online, every other renewal	not permitted 64 and older
Hawaii	8 years	2 years for people 72 and older	every renewal	every renewal	by mail, limited to 2 consecutive renewals	by mail, limited to 2 consecutive renewals
Idaho	4 or 8 years, personal option	4 years for people 63 and older	every renewal	every renewal	by mail, every other renewal; must choose 4-year license	not permitted 70 and older
Illinois	4 years	2 years for people 81 - 86; 1 year for people 87 and older	when renewing in person	75 and older, every renewal	both, every other renewal	not permitted 75 and older
Indiana	6 years	3 years for people 75-84; 2 years for people 85 and older	when renewing in person	75 and older, every renewal	online, every other renewal	not permitted 75 and older
Iowa	8 years or 74th birthday, whichever occurs first1	2 years for people 72 and older	when renewing in person	70 and older, every renewal	online, every other renewal	not permitted 70 and older

State	License Renewal for General Population	License Renewal for Older Population	Proof of Adequate Vision for General Population	Proof of Adequate Vision for Older Population	Mail or Online renewal permitted for General Population	Mail or Online renewal permitted for Older Population
Kansas	6 years	4 years for people 65 and older	every renewal	every renewal	no	no
Kentucky	4 years	4 years	no	no	no	no
Louisiana	6 years	6 years	when renewing in person	70 and older, every renewal	both, every other renewal	not permitted 70 and older2
Maine	6 years	4 years for people 65 and older	first renewal after 40 and every other renewal until 62	62 and older, every renewal	both, unless proof of vision required	not permitted 62 and older
Maryland	8 years	8 years	when renewing in person	40 and older, every renewal	both, every other renewal	both, every other renewal
Massachusetts	5 years	5 years	when renewing in person	75 and older, every renewal	online, every other renewal	not permitted 75 and older
Michigan	4 years	4 years	when renewing in person	when renewing in person	both, every other renewal	both, every other renewal
Minnesota	4 years	4 years	every renewal	every renewal	no	no
Mississippi	4 or 8 years, personal option	4 or 8 years, personal option	no	no	online, every other renewal	online, every other renewal
Missouri	6 years	3 years for people 70 and older	every renewal	every renewal	no	no
Montana	8 years or 75th birthday, whichever occurs first	4 years for people 75 and older	every renewal	every renewal	both, every other renewal (effective 01/01/17)	both, every other renewal (effective 01/01/17)
Nebraska	5 years	5 years	when renewing in person	72 and older, every renewal	online, every other renewal	not permitted 72 and older

State	License Renewal for General Population	License Renewal for Older Population	Proof of Adequate Vision for General Population	Proof of Adequate Vision for Older Population	Mail or Online renewal permitted for General Population	Mail or Online renewal permitted for Older Population
Nevada	4 years (odd number birth year); 8 years (even number birth year); 8 years all licenses starting in 2018	4 years for people 65 and older	when renewing in person	71 and older, every renewal	both, every other renewal; available only for holders of a 4-year license	both, every other renewal for people 65 and older
New Hampshire	5 years	5 years	every renewal	every renewal	online, every other renewal	online, every other renewal
New Jersey	4 years	2 or 4 years for people 70 and older, personal option	every 10 years3	every 10 years3	by mail, unless new photo required4	by mail, unless new photo required4
New Mexico	4 or 8 years, personal option	4 years for people 67-74; 1 year for people 75 and older	when renewing in person	75 and older, every renewal	online, every other renewal; by mail, unless new photo required	not permitted 75 and older
New York	8 years	8 years	every renewal	every renewal	both	both
North Carolina	8 years	5 years for people 66 and older	every renewal	every renewal	no	no
North Dakota	6 years	4 years for people 78 and older	every renewal	every renewal	no	no
Ohio	4 years	4 years	every renewal	every renewal	no	no
Oklahoma	4 years	4 years	no	no	no	no
Oregon	8 years	8 years	no	50 and older, every renewal	no	no
Pennsylvania	4 years	2 years or 4 years for people 65 and older, personal option	no	no	both	both
Rhode Island	5 years	2 years for people 75 and older	every renewal	every renewal	online, every other renewal	online, every other renewal
South Carolina	10 years	5 years for people 65 and older	every 5 years5	every 5 years5	by mail, for 5 years, every other renewal	by mail, for 5 years, every other renewal

State	License Renewal for General Population	License Renewal for Older Population	Proof of Adequate Vision for General Population	Proof of Adequate Vision for Older Population	Mail or Online renewal permitted for General Population	Mail or Online renewal permitted for Older Population
South Dakota	5 years	5 years	when renewing in person	65 and older, every renewal	both, every other renewal	both, every other renewal
Tennessee	8 years6	8 years6	no	no	both	both
Texas	6 years	2 years for people 85 and older	when renewing in person	79 and older, every renewal	both, every other renewal	not permitted 79 and older
Utah	5 years	5 years	when renewing in person	65 and older, every renewal	online, every other renewal	online, every other renewal
Vermont	2 or 4 years	2 or 4 years	no	no	by mail, unless new photo required7	by mail, unless new photo required7
Virginia	8 years	5 years for people 75 and older	when renewing in person	75 and older, every renewal	both, every other renewal	not permitted 75 and older
Washington	6 years	6 years	every renewal	every renewal	both, every other renewal	not permitted 70 and older
West Virginia	8 years	8 years	every renewal	every renewal	no	no
Wisconsin	8 years	8 years	every renewal	every renewal	no	no
Wyoming	4 years	4 years	every 8 years	every 8 years	by mail, every other renewal	by mail, every other renewal

The safety of your loved one and others is too valuable to ignore this important issue. Have the talk if you feel it is necessary!

Chapter 15- Social Media, Technology & the Internet
Eddie Morris

Every year our aging population watches more and more of their friends pass away or move to faraway nursing homes. Their health problems mean they often can't get around as well independently; their vision troubles make driving and reading a challenge. School goes back in session and their families are busy with all of their own extracurricular activities so even when they live close, the visits become fewer and rushed.

Grandparents are commonly anxious to stay involved in the bustling of life. Now whether it is talking face-to-face via Skype or just following updates and pictures on Facebook, technology is keeping more people in touch with their kids and actually involved in their grandkids' lives. Connecting with loved ones has never been easier and other technical innovations help with failed hearing, sight, memory and availing folks to tools so they can age in place (live at home) longer.

Family Connection

While some of us may grumble about having to learn how to use new electronic devices, a lot of technology can make our lives simpler and more fulfilling. Using the home computer as a cost-effective way to make phone calls and do video conferencing has got people talking by taking advantage of this form of communication. Because of the ease in getting it set up, many people are applying it to a variety of personal situations. Now, the tools that started as a means to pull people from around the world into online meetings are considered ordinary for people to connect with family and friends.

The Pew Research Center's Internet and American Life Project ("Pew Research Center's Internet and American Life Project") tracked adults using online video technology. They found that 31% of people 50 years old and older are using this form of communication. Half of that 31% were 65 and older. Even just getting started using technology is a bonding experience between generations. The know-how is straightforward and many teenagers are quite capable of helping their grandparents get setup.

These real-time connections with family are an advantage. Grandparents can place a call and read books to their grandchildren at bedtime, share in the excitement of a report card, admire a new baby or view a newly completed school project. Imagine being able to show your grandchildren one of your special talents such as knitting or woodcarving without having to travel to show them. How meaningful for them and you to be able to share your lives with each other on a regular basis.

Health Care Management

According to an article in the New York Times, a woman, age 100, who is a resident at an assisted-living center in North Carolina, got assistance from her geriatric care manager to connect her with her grandson, who was a six-hour drive away, while she was at her doctor's appointment. Via a web cam and a laptop computer with a link to Skype, her grandson could see what was happening at the doctor's appointment and engage in the care at the moment it was being given. What a way to erase the miles between families during such fundamental moments in life.

In another illustration, an ABC news report told about how Dr. Loren Olson, a psychiatrist from Iowa, shared how his experience with Skype changed the way he works. Dr. Olson began using Skype for making calls to his grandchildren and then realized that he could use it for routine follow up 'med-check' visits with both city and rural patients. He could also conduct clinical consultations with a team of medical providers in a rural area. He shared that his "patients have responded quite well…some even preferring this method of care. The patients tend to become totally absorbed and relaxed in the discussion such that the technology literally melts away. While it can't replace the office visit, it does create access to care that has not been available before."

Fighting Depression and Loneliness

Many Seniors have long ago left the neighborhood where they laid down roots so social structures like close extended families, neighborhood groups and religious institutions aren't as strong or as readily available as they were for their counterparts of 50 years ago. Life events like caring for a sick spouse, leaving the workforce and the passing of loved ones, friends and peers can quickly become problematic when the remains of their now familiar social networks become threatened.

Increasing reports discuss the high rate of loneliness among seniors (one study showed that 40 percent of adults over age 65 are chronically lonely) and other studies found a link between chronic loneliness and various health risks. According to a study published by Brigham Young University) loneliness and social isolation are just as much a threat to longevity as obesity, something that public health takes very seriously," said Julianne Holt-Lunstad, the lead study author. "We need to start taking our social relationships more seriously." This study suggests that the risk for mortality actually surpasses health risks associated with obesity and heavy smoking. Although loneliness and social isolation are very different in definition, according to this study the effect on longevity is still much the same for those two scenarios.

The good news is that technology can connect folks to loved ones, support groups, and people with similar interests therefore fighting back depression. According to this BYU study, the more positive mindset we keep in our world, the better we are able to function not just emotionally but physically and that there are many things that help to subdue the effects of loneliness.

The Men of the Harvard Grant Study is based on one of the longest studies of aging in the world. It began in 1938 and tracked the physical and emotional health of 268 Harvard students (dozens of whom survived into their 90s.) The study shows that relationships are the key to healthy aging, said Dr. Vaillant, the man who led the study for more than 40 years. He advised cultivating younger friends for their energy and fresh perspective. "You must have somebody outside yourself to be interested in — not hobbies or crossword puzzles or your stock account — but flesh and blood," he said. With the evolution of the internet, people can stay in contact over long distances like they never could before. Many retirement communities, senior centers and public libraries across the country now offer basic computer and internet courses.

Hearing and Sight

Technology is continually advancing tools that provide incoming and outgoing voice amplification, larger buttons or buttons with pictures on them, caller identification, memory dial, speakers, alerting devices and other programmable options to improve telephone communication. If you are one of the 65+ seniors who text on their cell phones, mobiles such as the Jitterbug Touch come with a slide-out keyboard and touchscreen for fingers that aren't so dexterous anymore.

Companies like CapTel (Captioned Telephone) offer hardwired telephones that print out the words as the caller is saying them, so there is no confusion for those who can't make out every word of a phone call. For seniors who do not have computers and aren't interested, videophones, an old technology (from the 1950s) are like telephones that have built-in cameras and a video screen. You need an Internet connection like DSL or cable; however, videophones are particularly useful for the deaf and speech-impaired who use sign language or find the visual images helpful in understanding the conversation.

Claria Zoom is an Android smartphone app for low vision available from GooglePlay, "the interface with very large characters and contrasted colors allows you to both adapt your phone to your sight and easily access all the functionalities available. You can then send text messages, read your emails and favorite newspapers, but also use dedicated tools such as the magnifier or the OCR (Optical character recognition).

E-Books readers (like Kindles) have typeset that is adjustable so it can make reading easier for eyes that no longer work as well as they once did. Many libraries offer eBooks as part of their loaner services. To upsell the online book options, there is even a program called Readeo that lets you read books with your grandkids over the computer. It uses a Skype-like video chat to let you and your grandkids choose from more than 200 children's books and read the book together, even if you are miles apart. During a "BookChat," the pages of the story appear on the computer screen and you can see, hear and talk to one another through video chat windows at the bottom of the screen.

Memory Aids

Believe it not, technology can even help strengthen your memory. Many digital devices and now even smart phones include memory aid tools which allow the user to record reminders about appointments, tasks, medication and so forth.

One memory aid that is actually fun is a video game. It is not just for your grandson anymore. Happier at Home reports that video games "tend to emphasize skills that are vulnerable to aging (speed, attention, memory, etc.). Thus, video games may offer the opportunity to get 'exercise' in areas that need it most. In addition, video games are novel for most senior adults and research suggests that this newness is an important ingredient for successful cognitive intervention."

Games that challenge your brain on the computer include video-game systems like the Wii, handheld video-game devices like the Nintendo DS and brain training websites like Lumosity.

Aging in Place Technology

Baby boomers are becoming seniors (age 65) at the rate of 10,000 per day, and not surprisingly, most of them want to do it from the comfort of their own home. Technology can help and interested parties everywhere are looking for ways to build a bridge between the resources and the consumers.

"Recent advances in technology are providing new options for seniors and their families that can allow them to remain at home longer by monitoring health status, detecting emergency situations and notifying health care providers about any changes in health status," Senator Claire McCaskill (D-Missouri), the ranking member of the committee, said in her opening statement in May 2015 to the U.S. Senate. "These technologies can also make family members' and caregivers' lives easier by providing them with tools to support their loved ones and giving them peace of mind. This really is a win-win situation, seniors are much happier continuing their normal routines and social activities where they feel comfortable, family members can make sure their loved ones are safe. At the same time society benefits from significantly reduced healthcare and long-term care costs."

Vendors have developed bed and chair exit sensors that warn caregivers when patients leave or attempt to leave their beds, digital pill dispensers that can be locked until it is time for medication, devices that monitor when seniors take falls at home and platforms to keep family members and caregivers up-to-date via check-ins, medication notifications and routine deviation monitoring.

Closing

Technology can truly enrich lives. Using the internet for social media and technology resources can:

> ➤ Keep friends and families connected
> ➤ Provide an avenue to manage Health Care remotely
> ➤ Tackle Depression and Loneliness
> ➤ Enhance Hearing and Sight
> ➤ Strengthen Memory, and

> ➤ Keep people in their homes longer while giving great peace of mind to those who care.

It makes life easier, which in turn should empower you when it becomes a struggle to do things the way that you've always done them. As needs change, a simple search on the internet can introduce you to what is new in the realm of growing old and aging in place.

Works Cited

1. *http://www.pewinternet.org/~/media/Files/Reports/2010/PIP_Video calling data memo.pdf.* (n.d.).

2. *http://newoldage.blogs.nytimes.com/2010/05/27/screen-time-with-mom/.* (n.d.).

3. *http://abcnews.go.com/video/playerIndex?id=7530334.* (n.d.).

4. *http://assets.aarp.org/rgcenter/general/loneliness_2010.pdf.* (n.d.).

5. *http://news.byu.edu/archive15-mar-loneliness.aspx.* (n.d.).

6. *http://archinte.jamanetwork.com/article.aspx?articleid=1188033.* (n.d.).

7. *http://www.happierathome.org/the-latest-in-technology-to-fight-memory-loss.* (n.d.).

Chapter 16- Managing Their Schedule and Yours
Margaret Maczulski

You have a life. You have family and people and contacts and commitments. You may have a job or activities that take up a major part of your day. Others may rely on you in varying degrees to help them with things in their lives. That's the way it works. If you become the primary family caregiver for aging parents, then you need to prepare yourself. You could potentially add 100% more of your committable time to helping a parent(s) or a loved one to function in their daily lives. It is possible that for a period in your life there may not be much "free time" for a long, long time. Trying to manage your own life schedule while assisting aging parents with theirs can be so simple and yet so complex. Your senior loved ones need your help now just like they helped you earlier in your life.

As we age, we evolve and life becomes different. One obvious change is that usually seniors retire and no longer have a full time job, or have a limited and different workload. The repercussions of not having a "normal" work schedule can be significant. One no longer needs to be at a certain place at a certain time and return home after hours away to relax for the evening. The structure of their life, or lack thereof, becomes more flexible.

Some have problems with this void and may become lethargic and depressed and even ill. Others take on a new adventure and make adjustments accordingly. The observable fact is that nearly everyone tends to slow down. The body gets older and does not respond as quickly as one has become accustomed to being throughout a lifetime. We aren't as strong as we once were. Nor is the hearing and eyesight as acute. Whereas once a walking stride was quick and brisk, it is now slower and plodding.

Your lives will be easier, albeit busier if you make an effort to be organized for you and your loved ones. This means living around scheduling. Confusion can be very frustrating but there are ways to keep things moving along and on target with schedules. The more you can keep your loved one interested in making their own plans the better everyone will function. But there comes a time when they no longer remember things well or cannot drive anymore and that's when their tasks become more yours.

Hopefully every member of your family will pitch in and be responsible for certain tasks of your loved one. But realistically, it is usually one or two family members who bear the greatest share of caring for their seniors. To make your life as easy as possible, start by making a schedule:

- ➢ Make it for a week, Sunday through Saturday
- ➢ Be organized when setting up your schedule, and keep it simple.
- ➢ Start with your daily activities and prioritize the activities that are:
  - o Critical
  - o Important
  - o Elective
  - o Occasional
  - o One-time occurrence

Suggestion: Start with a spreadsheet with the days of the week across the top and the activities in a column along the left side of the document. Mark the times that each activity occurs on the appropriate day.

	S	M	T	W	TH	F	S
AWAKE	8 AM	7 AM	7 AM	7 AM	7 AM	7 AM	8 AM
DRESS	9 AM						
BREAKFAST	9 AM						
WORK							
LUNCH							
WORK							
ERRANDS							

Add more activities as needed. Keep the times as specific and accurate as possible. Then make a similar schedule for your loved one(s). Then make a schedule for anyone else who will be directly involved in the support with your loved one.

Next compare the times and determine when there are opportunities (free times) to interject your loved one's scheduled tasks into your own (or others). Look for times that might be geographically easier to combine activities. Examples might be activities like:

- ➢ Running an errand for mom during a lunch break from work
- ➢ Or maybe stopping by your mom to make sure she takes her meds correctly and eats breakfast before you go to work

If you can't do it, hire a caregiver who you manage, to do these type of tasks:

- ➤ Medication reminders
- ➤ Personal hygiene including bathing or showering, toileting and dressing
- ➤ Meal preparation whether it be cooking or organizing what foods will be included in your loved ones' diet
- ➤ Housekeeping such as vacuuming and doing the laundry
- ➤ Running errands
- ➤ Going to doctor appointments
- ➤ Driving
- ➤ Exercising
- ➤ Laughing and conversation

You will still be involved if you hire someone to care for your loved one but it will relieve the constant pressure of doing it alone. Having someone who is a backup relieves the pressure of always being available even for unplanned events.

These schedules will give you a point of reference to start your discussion of when you and other family members will need to be available to assist your loved one with everything, or conversely let your seniors manage themselves in coordination with you.

Your loved one will likely be most comfortable with incorporating the relevant items then into a big calendar (or white board that has squares like a month on a calendar) where you can write scheduled doctor's appointments and special events. Determine how those appointments can best be handled. Is there a day, or an afternoon, that you can allocate to picking up; driving; being present at the appointment; then drive your loved one home and make sure that they have a good meal and will be comfortable and able to go to bed without incident.

It often takes an emergency stay in a hospital to finally determine the responsibilities of Power of Attorney for Finances and Power of Attorney for Medical. How about the finances?

Usually one child will manage the checkbook, or at least review the bills that are paid. It is an important role and takes time. To whom is your loved one writing checks? There are thieves who prey upon the sympathy from  seniors. Do not be fooled and keep up with alerts from their County States Attorney Office who can help you with questions and situations. Contact them!

Additionally, all the investments; wills and trusts must be current and up to date. It can really mean a lot of time contacting banks; attorneys and financial institutions to say nothing of extended family members and any other interested parties (committable charities and pledges).

The Medical Power of Attorney has different challenges. To start, they must address if the loved one has a current DNR (Do Not Resuscitate). Each state is different but it gives the subject the opportunity to choose if they want to be resuscitated and potentially put on live support in a life-threatening situation. HIPAA forms must be current in order to give and gain access to medical information. Making sure that a Living Will is in place is important.

Keeping everything in a safe, central place in the home is important. There will be papers; documents; lists; notebooks and tools that you and everyone will use and need to know where they are. Keep it simple. Of course, there may be items which need to be kept elsewhere such as banking and financial institutions. Make a list of these, keep it in the central place and make sure that it is up to date.

Make lists and share your lists with complete contact information. Keep the lists together with all the important documents in the home. They can include (but are not limited to) everything from:

> Doctors
> Therapists
> Medication
> Insurance
> Friends
> Family
> Business Contacts
> Banks
> Valuables like jewelry and art
> Organizations
> Utilities
> Regular Appointments
> Diet and Groceries
> Regular Tasks
> Power of Attorney Financial and Power of Attorney Medical

Determine and stay within a timeframe for all tasks and make decisions. If a decision is wrong the first time, make the change but always move forward. Indecisiveness will only cause frustration and confusion.

So much of what we do these days is through technology that our loved ones may or may not embrace. Particularly difficult is using a phone system of answering questions to computer generated voice systems. Everything is being directed to websites for a "self-serve" system to answer questions, make changes and resolve problems. This can be enormously helpful to you if you are computer savvy and can quickly clear up a loved one's problem before they become too big to handle.

Many families set up a personal account and use social media to convey information quickly and easily to family members in order to keep everyone informed. If decisions need to be made jointly, this is a good method to communicate. But everyone must be on board or opted out, or make their own concerted effort then to keep informed. This can also serve as a form of a diary of actions being taken by whom and when.

Making a schedule is easy. Making it work well for everyone will take time and effort. But it will save you many frustrating moments. Sudden and unexpected occurrences will happen so prepare for what you do know.

Make Useful Schedules

- ➢ Use a calendar
- ➢ Keep everything in one safe place in the home
- ➢ Make lists
- ➢ Write everything down
- ➢ Keep to a schedule
- ➢ Keep to a timeframe
- ➢ Be efficient but kind
- ➢ Make decisions
- ➢ Share information on social media or what works best for you

They helped you to grow up and be the person that you are. Help them to be comfortable and safe in their senior years. They have a life too and they will love you forever.

Chapter 17- Family Conversations- Keeping People in the Know
William Bruck

Conversation in the Realm of Homecare Communication- Caregivers, Clients and Clans

Let us begin by saying, the leading difficulty with communication is the lack of communication and the key hindrance to getting a point across, is failure to get the point across. These two thoughts may seem naive and petty, but they describe the root issues with the lack of real, meaningful, purposeful communication: defining the sender, the receiver, the message, and staying on topic.

Now if it was all this easy, I could end the chapter right here. However, once we include all the other factors mentioned above, and countless others, we are forced to study the issue a little deeper. When communication takes place in the realm of homecare, conversations are generally never between one sender and one receiver. When homecare is involved, it generally involves an entire family or families which require a sender to simultaneously communicate with multiple receivers at the same time! Many of these individuals within the family structure have various priorities of values and scale, differing levels of responsibility and every family has a variety of dynamics that make it individually unique. One key to successful communication in homecare is to break down barriers or avoid them altogether.

When initially going into a home to discuss care options, there is a chance that the message about to received, may not be received as a need. Certain parties may even be hostile to the thought of it. There must be a cordial proper introduction between the receiver and the sender prior to any message being sent. A good receiver must be relaxed, receptive, and responsive. If not properly prepared, successful communication may not be possible. Home care discussions take on their own unique set of dynamics that must be recognized, planned for and understood in order for successful communication to take place.

Communication has three main components: a sender, a receiver and a message. Added to this are many other factors including: attitudes, distractions, white noise, misconceptions/misunderstandings, unfocused message, body language, preconceived biases/thoughts, and confusion of who the receiver should be. The key to beneficial communication lies in a prepared sender sending a clear concise defined message to a prepared needful receiver. One must also discern three things: who is the decision maker, what/who is the biggest barrier to communication, what is the highest concern of the potential client/ elderly person to whom care is desired?

A message has been compared to the water flowing in a stream. It may appear that flow is occurring, but there are also many hindrances to that perceived flow. Within the creek bed are rocks, sticks, fish, frogs, otters, and the occasional child interrupting the water's seemingly calm flow. To say the water flows seamlessly and is a simple process would be an understatement. The surface of the water is just the surface of the message. Beneath are so many other factors that create the stream into something alive and vibrant and sometimes incoherent as well.

A seemingly good message can be easily altered by a single factor thrown in. The crucial point is to maintain the integrity of the message so it does not get overlooked by the babbling as a result of the rocks on the shore.

When planning a conversation, start with a plan. When starting a conversation, follow a plan. When in the middle of a conversation, return to the plan. When ending a conversation, fulfill the plan. No one conversation is ever the same, but each one should be approached similarly and with a similar overall plan for success.

As a 24-year Veteran of the military (Army to be exact), I like to place situations into a military matrix that allows me to analyze, compartmentalize and address issues in order to be successful. In the military, success is gauged on conquering or meeting an objective. In the context of communication, the objective is "getting the intended message to the intended receiver" and if this goal is met then success is gained. In the military there are many ways to conquer an objective. The first part of the planning process is to define your objective and the various individuals and organizations you must deal with in order to meet that objective. In the military different maneuvers can be utilized, such as flanking, envelopment, bypass and frontal approaches.

In no way am I proposing that homecare discussions should be approached in a regimented military manner. However, I am advocating the fact that successful communication involves a great deal of tact, planning, and strategy because no one approach fits all scenarios.

Sometimes understanding the goal allows the sender to use a strategy with multiple family members that bypasses hang-ups and irritations in order to get the intended message across. It may be an upfront blatant approach would not be best, while at other times flanking influential family members would not be the wisest avenue of approach, but bypassing a particular item may be the correct choice.

Remember the outcome is not the battle but it is the success of meeting, or the failure to meet the desired goal. If the goal is getting "x" amount of hours of care per week to help mom or dad, then "x" should not be the ultimate goal, but care in the home for mom should be. I have personally seen verbal explosions over the issue of "every day of the week" care is a must. Mom may put up a huge defensive wall up to "every day of the week", but if the goal is "care in the home" I recommend aiming small with the intention of expanding as time allows. Stick with an attainable, realistic, and acceptable goal and conquer it!

No matter where the conversation goes, the potential client must be made part of the conversation. Also, the individual who makes the final decision must not be lost in the conversation. Initially the one to whom care is being discussed will have an apprehensive mindset and may even feel slighted over the mere discussion of "unnecessary help" coming into her/his home. The plan should include a sub-goal of placing the elderly individual at ease. This can be accomplished through a variety of actions and questions. Questions such as, "what would make you comfortable?" or "how would you feel about...?" can be very valuable. Within the context on the conversation, maintain eye contact with the individual as well as turning one's body toward them when speaking to them. Do not use flamboyant hand gestures or walk around the room while speaking. Maintain a calm reserved demeanor that presents a sincere, thought-out and well executed plan. When speaking, speak clearly, define terms within the context, and tailor the conversation to avoid known pressure points or bottlenecks. General rule of thumb, in the homecare discussion, there is one or two family members who are resistive to a "stranger" coming into the home. Sometimes the barrier to successful communication is the potential client, but often it is a family member or friend who interjects themselves to oversee the plan of care. If an issue does arise during a conversation, address the issue, avoid placing undue emphasis on the issue and as quickly as possible get back on topic.

Always respect the home. While in the home, the elder individual is king/queen. Treat the individual with the upmost respect and admiration. Compliment the home and the owner, and respect the authority (whether the individual actually has it or not) of the potential client. Understand and sympathize with the family that a stranger will be entering the home and that there is a great deal of natural apprehension. Create easy transitions to this topic with through comprehensive descriptions of caregivers who may possibly enter the home.

At times, members of a family may create "white noise", at times these distractions seemingly hinder getting to the goal. However, trivial questions still need to be addressed. Do not spend a great amount of time on these side issues and quickly restructure the conversation back to the preconceived plan for the meeting. The goal is to create "peace of mind" for all the receiver's, as well as confidence that you are not minimalizing issues but still maintain control over the conversation. A light trivial story or a personal example can oftentimes defuse a real conflict as a last resort.

Remain flexible during the whole communication process. If you feel it is going in a wrong direction, take charge and redirect it back toward the message intended. Always be the expert, but also be capable of understanding for the feelings, wishes, and desires of others. In the end you may not necessarily make every family member entirely satisfied, but also understand that not every issue must be dealt with completely or overcome in any one particular conversation. If necessary, take time to regroup, gather more information and at the very least, be more prepared for the next conversation regarding homecare.

Communication as a stand-alone skill is hard enough. Each scenario creates different circumstances and difficulties for getting a message across. We communicate differently when at work, home, church, rotary, restaurants, etc. understanding the basics of communication is foundational to success. Each family has its own set of conditions, which distort the conduit of the message of homecare. Understand that the proposition is not a naturally comfortable one, and that one singular individual must ultimately be the decision maker or the final deal maker in order for it to begin. The message (goal) must be clearly definable and professionally advanced. The receiver must be respected and defused.

Lastly, the sender must be honest and authoritative in both delivery and plan, and responsive to changes that are most certain to occur.
If one fails to set a goal, with certainty it will never be met.

Chapter 18- Funeral & Final Wishes
Eddie Morris

Did you know that Singer Janis Joplin, who died at the young age of 27, managed to update her will only two days before her death? She provided for up to $2,500 to be set aside for a party in her honor.

As an owner of an Agency who cares for folks at the end of their life, I am often addressing the issue of mortality. One of life's guarantees is death and yet many people do not leave any type of verbal or written instructions for their loved ones to follow after that event.

I am not just referring to instructions about what they would want to happen to their property (which should be written down in a last will and testament or a living trust) but details of what type of funeral arrangements they would want and what should happen to their remains after they're gone go unmentioned. Parents pick a song or a burial spot then think that is all they need to manage because their kids or spouse will "just know" how to memorialize them. What they fail to think through is that they and their spouse may be in an accident together forcing the kids to think through life and death decisions all at once during a time of high emotions or that the kids may all have differing ideas of what is "right" when the time comes to make decisions – again at a time of high emotions.

Off the top of your head, how quickly can you identify answers to this list of your personal information?

> Birth date and social security number
> Group of people and or organizations needing to be contacted if something happens to you
> Executor or primary beneficiary
> Church or place of worship / Pastor or other religious contact
> Someone to care for your home and pets, if any
> Information about preplanned services
> If unplanned, funeral home preferred
> Final resting place
> All memorial wishes, and where they should be sent
> Preferences of burial clothing, jewelry, or special items
> Musical preferences, if any

- ➤ People selected as pall bearers
- ➤ Special acknowledgment of family members and friends at service
- ➤ Floral preference
- ➤ Reading for the service
- ➤ Special requests or prayers
- ➤ Will / Durable Power of Attorney
- ➤ Checking and/or Saving account info
- ➤ Retirement accounts
- ➤ Bank statements, property deeds and other financial records
- ➤ Marriage certificate
- ➤ Military discharge papers
- ➤ Insurance policies
- ➤ Tax returns
- ➤ Mortgages
- ➤ Charge accounts
- ➤ Other current bills
- ➤ Automobile title and registration

Now, do you know all those answers for your spouse? Or do you know anyone who can easily tackle this list if your spouse passes with you? Now let's imagine that you or your loved one has to identify this information while dealing with the emotional impact of loss.

Do you want a Body burial?
- ➤ Costs depend on the casket selected, the services provided by the mortician, and the charges made by the cemetery; the grave site, the vault or liner, opening and closing the grave, the marker or monument, and perpetual care. Costs could range from $800 to well over $5,000)

Do you want a Cremation?
- ➤ It is increasingly popular. It accomplishes in a few hours what nature takes years to complete. A modest container, rather than an expensive casket is generally used, and total costs range from about $200 to well over $1,000. Many crematories

will work directly with a family for substantial savings, but all permits must be in order, accompanied by a death certificate.

- ➤ Cremated remains (cremains) may be scattered, buried, or stored in an urn. They can be easily transported or inexpensively shipped. Their disposition can be handled by the next of kin or a designee. Although some denominations oppose cremation, the majority accept it.

Do you want a Bequeathal?

- ➤ Bequeathing your body to a medical school is another option. Many medical schools value a body for teaching or research purposes and may pay for transportation and final disposition, usually cremation. If requested, some medical colleges will return the cremains to the family for disposition.

- ➤ It is important to have a written agreement with a medical school, and it is essential to have alternative plans. The circumstances of your death may render your body unacceptable for teaching purposes. Autopsies are valuable for medical science, and organ transplants give priceless benefits to recipients. Most medical schools do not accept a body on which an autopsy has been performed or from which organs (other than corneas) have been removed.

Aside from the disposition of your body, there is the question of the kind of service you prefer. Should it be formal or informal? Public or private?

Do you want a funeral?

- ➤ A funeral service is one with the body present. Therefore, it is held soon after death occurs, generally in a religious setting or mortuary. There is also the option, as in days past, to have a funeral at your own or family home.

Do you want a committal or memorial service?

> A committal service may be held at the graveside immediately before burial or in a crematory chapel before cremation.

> A memorial service is held without the body present and does not require extensive services or the expense of a mortician. It can be scheduled several days, weeks, or even months after death occurs. This allows time for far-away family or friends to gather. It also allows those who loved you to choose the most appropriate way to celebrate your life and what you meant to them, separate from the initial grief, when they have had time to reflect and grieve.

When a person passes, there are two tasks at hand. The first is the timely disposition of the body. The other is celebrating the life that was lived. When you can separate those two events, there will be more likelihood of saving stress and money.

For many people, a funeral is one of the largest expenses they will face. Today, funerals often cost $8,000 or more. Most people will make final arrangements having little knowledge of their rights or alternatives. Decisions are made at a time when people are most vulnerable and their judgment is clouded by grief and bereavement. They may feel that the monetary amount spent on final arrangements measures and expresses just how much they loved you.

Take a moment to consider how taking that decision upon yourself could ease the way for those you leave behind.

> ➤ Planning ahead can be satisfying for people who like to make their own decisions and do things for themselves. It gives them a feeling of responsibility for themselves, and for others.

> ➤ Knowing arrangements are made eases some worries about dying or burdening others with unfinished business.

> ➤ People can explore alternatives and make choices that suit their personal choices, religious beliefs, and finances.

> ➤ Planning gives people an important opportunity to help others with anatomical donations or memorial gifts to a favorite charity. It also saves families all of the difficulty and pain that can arise over making these decisions during the time of crisis.

> ➤ Planning ahead does not mean paying ahead but it can save money. It also protects loved ones from emotional mistakes and expensive decisions when death occurs.

Thinking through and detailing the specifics ahead of time is a kind way to ensure that your loved ones are clear on what your preferences are and you will likely save them great frustration so they can properly remember you during a time when they are mourning your presence deeply.

In summarizing this chapter, I've included a list of 4 tips to follow to make your final wishes known to your loved ones:

Tips for Making Your Final Wishes Known

1. Do not make your will or trust the only place where you write down your funeral wishes. While your last will and testament or living trust is the place where you should write down what you want to happen to your property after you die and who should be in charge of making sure that your property goes where you want it to go, your will or trust should not be the only place where you list your funeral wishes. Why not? Because usually by the time your will or trust is located and read, your loved ones will have already made all of the decisions about the disposition of your remains (burial or cremation) and memorial, if any.

2. The best way to let your loved ones know about your funeral wishes is to write down a list of specific instructions in a document that is separate from your will or trust. This separate document should include whether you want a funeral or memorial service and where; whether you want a gathering of friends and family and where; whether you want to be cremated, and, if so, where you would like your ashes to stored or disposed of; and if you want to be buried and where. Having conversations about funeral plans are often considered morbid and thus difficult with loved ones. But it is relatively easy to let your loved ones know in passing that you have created a "just in case" document and tell them where it is stored so that they can access it at the appropriate time.

3. Use an online service to document your funeral wishes. In this day and age pretty much anything can be found on the internet, and this includes websites for documenting and storing your funeral wishes as well as your will or trust and other estate planning documents. Some of these websites will even allow you to create messages that will be emailed after you die. Check out AgingWithDignity.org, Parting Wishes, My Last Song - Lifebox, and Funeral Inspirations.

4. If you are really not inclined to write down your final wishes or document them online, then please consider talking to your loved ones about your final wishes. It could be as simple as saying that

you would never want to be buried, or you would never want to be cremated. This will go a long way to ease stress and anxiety during a difficult time and give your loves ones a general idea about idea about what you would want, and not want.

Whatever your final wishes are, they are your last wishes and should be honored. By taking some time now to plan ahead, you can all but ensure that they will be honored. By the same token, make sure that you name someone you believe will honor your wishes as the executor of your Last Will and Testament. This individual will have a great degree of influence & control over legal issues and other important issues following your death.

If you cannot afford to pre-pay for your funeral, make a funeral wish list. Include all the details that are important to you. Although not legally binding, it is a way to express to your family members and loved ones how important your wishes are to you. Be sure to tell someone where these funeral-related documents are so that they can be easily located when needed.

When you make a will or purchase insurance, you are planning for your death and the lives of your survivors. By planning your final arrangements, you are doing precisely the same thing: smoothing the way for your survivors.

PART 3- HELPFUL HINTS

Chapter 19- Money Saving Tips for Seniors and Their Families
David Forman

From basic living expenses, to the specific needs of seniors, costs of nearly all the basic necessities of life have risen dramatically over the past few years. Unfortunately, in most US cities the populations among the least able to afford it are those living on a fixed income - disabled and elderly adults.

Making matters worse (which isn't a bad tagline for the federal government), the Social Security office announced that there would be no Cost of Living Increase (COLA) to Social Security benefits in 2016; a formula closely tied to the Federal Consumer Price Index (CPI). The complicated formula accounts for many consumer prices, but often lacks the cost of goods and spending habits most closely related to the needs of seniors and disabled adults.

Particularly in election years it is notable that this lack of increase in COLA to benefits, has occurred only four times since congressional law provided for an automatic increase since the law's inception in 1975, all of which occurred under the under the Obama administration. (See evidentiary chart, next page).

Perhaps the Social Security office (www.ssa.gov) the Agency responsible for COLA decisions, might consider my "tongue in cheek" proposal to sell branded merchandise to help their own financial woes.

The United States Federal Government

Making Matters Worse. It's What We do.

CPI includes various economic indicators and spending patterns among differing populations, but many economists point to deep flaws in the final calculations that do not account for the neediest groups. For example, while the lack of increase may be partially attributed to lower energy costs in 2016, most seniors and disabled adults do not receive much benefit from the lower fuel costs that were variables in the COLA calculation, simply because at 80 to 90 years old, most are not driving. In short, the people groups already struggling the most aren't helped much by lower gas prices if they do not drive.

According to World News Report (October, 2015) commenting on the lack of any Cost of Living Adjustment seniors would be hit the hardest and this prescient prediction came true. There were no cost of living benefit increases for 2016, while the costs of basic food staples like milk and eggs, and especially an exponential increase in the cost of prescription medications continued to rise.

This created more of a gap between what goods and services cost, and an ever-increasing disparity between what is covered by Medicaid Part 2 (an average of 80% of medical bills) and copays for prescriptions.

Social Security Cost-Of-Living Adjustments

Year	COLA	Year	COLA	Year	COLA
1975	8.0	1990	5.4	2005	4.1
1976	6.4	1991	3.7	2006	3.3
1977	5.9	1992	3.0	2007	2.3
1978	6.5	1993	2.6	2008	5.8
1979	9.9	1994	2.8	2009	0.0
1980	14.3	1995	2.6	2010	0.0
1981	11.2	1996	2.9	2011	3.6
1982	7.4	1997	2.1	2012	1.7
1983	3.5	1998	1.3	2013	1.5
1984	3.5	1999 *	2.5	2014	1.7
1985	3.1	2000	3.5	2015	0.0
1986	1.3	2001	2.6	2016	0.0
1987	4.2	2002	1.4	*Benefit increase to meet Cost of Living failed only four times in 42 years, all under the Obama administration*	
1988	4.0	2003	2.1		
1989	4.7	2004	2.7		

Reprinted from the official Social Security web site -
ettps://www.ssa.gov/news/cola/

Take Heart, The Cumulative Wisdom of Millions of Seniors Is Available Right Here to Help Stay Ahead of Rising Costs

More than 65 million Americans will receive almost 670 billion dollars in benefits in 2016, but among the millions who will struggle with increased costs, much creativity has been gained from sharing the collective ideas of thousands of seniors and their families. Remember, you are not alone in your frustration. You can save a substantial amount of money by considering what many have learned out of necessity.

Care Recipients, Families and Caregivers Should Take Some Time to Consider Recurring Expenses and Identify Those You May Be Willing to Sacrifice or Reduce.

Family caregivers should take some time to look at some of your expenses, or help mom or dad review theirs. A good place to start is with a previous month's bank statement. Gather utility bills and any recurring monthly items. Exact numbers aren't important at this time; you are simply looking for ways to save on the things that you are already paying for.

Bundle Services

Many seniors are still paying separate bills for local and long distance telephone and cable or satellite television. Today's bundled packages can be substantially less expensive, but competing ads and too much information can be confusing and intimidating. Help navigate through the best packages and switch to a single provider if it makes sense.   Do not worry about long hold times and long menus to choose from, the "sales" departments of most major service providers answer far quicker than you may be remembering the last time you tried to call with a billing or service issue.

Many of us over the age of 60 are attached to landline phones and digital answering machines. These days, the power in your home is more likely to go down than a loss in cell service because of the redundancy of the systems in place for cell service. If you live in an area with clear signals, your landlines are obsolete, and your cell's voicemail is as easy to use as any separate answering machine.

Insurance companies offer deep discounts for multiple policies. Switching to a single provider for auto and home for example can save hundreds of dollars per year. Search for monthly charges that can be replaced by one-time charges.

Medical alert alarms can be lifesaving, but most come with a costly monthly monitoring fee. Look for a personal alarm system that can connect directly to 911 with no monitoring fees and no service contracts.

In the car, "On Star" is a nice luxury but also comes with a costly monthly fee. A basic GPS device from Garmin or TOMTOM has a onetime cost of about $79 and speaks the same directions out loud. Even better, most smart phones have GPS and map directions. Set your destination before you even get into the car, and you are on your way anywhere without extra cost. Use voice readout when your phone screen is too small to see while driving.

Shop Locally
Your trip to the grocery store and back may be adding $5 or more per trip! Dollar General stores are proliferating throughout the United States, they may be closer than your grocery store and you'll notice lower prices on just about every item.

Compare
Competition is great for consumers and most people live within driving distance of two, three or more grocery stores, plus discount stores and "Big Box" stores. Some stores are more expensive and make no effort to hide it. Trader Joes, Whole Foods and others have a luxury niche market for people who feel good by spending more unnecessarily for words like "organic, natural, grass-fed, cage-free etc." God bless them, but head for Walmart. Bring a pad and paper, choose a half-dozen items that you buy often and write down their prices (do not forget unit-cost, as well as price in order to make the correct comparison). For the purpose of this experiment, do not write down items that are on sale. Leave the pad in your car, and choose a different store the next time you shop. Find the same items (not on sale) and note their prices. Do this for a number of

stores in your area, and you may be completely amazed at the cost difference. A couple of dollars' savings on several items, quickly add up to huge savings from one store over another.

Do not fall for it! Lately stores have resumed an old marketing trick, and many are falling for it. Promotions that ask that you buy more than you intended for a supposed cost savings can be very costly at checkout. For example, let's say Chips at your favorite store are $2.50 each with a large, brightly colored tag that says Buy 5 bags for $10. What just happened? Did you buy five and save $2.50? Sure that's one way to look at it (The way your store hopes you will), or did you just spend $7.50 more than you intended to spend this trip? This was a simple example, but next time you go shopping, take a closer look at how your favorite store(s) are pricing items with a goal of having you spend far more at checkout than you normally would have. When you identify the worst offenders, find another favorite store.

Coupon Shopping

For some it is almost an addiction, but for most it is a hassle. If you enjoy clipping newspaper coupons, find your own way to organize them by brand or product type to make them easy to find at the right time. Most people will use far less than half the coupons they "clip." Online coupon and discount sites are more efficient. Rather than hoping this week's specials match your desires, an easy to use coupon site online will find savings by brand or product at your favorite store. Next time you shop; you'll use closer to 100% of the coupons you brought. Just Google "Grocery Coupons" and you'll find a web site that's best for you.

In addition to national sites like coupons.com or mygrocerydeals.com, try the name of the store where you shop, there you'll also find all of the store's promotions, like saving points for lower gas prices, or other cost-saving benefits. Members of Circleofmoms.com a web site that often shares money saving tips for families, claim savings of $200 or more on groceries each month. Some national statistics suggest the average shopper's coupon savings on groceries is about 15% annually. With an average cost of groceries at $500 to $1,000 per month, that translates to $900 to $1,800 per year in savings!

Those who regularly use coupons, or "extreme couponers," say they aim to save at least 50% or more, which amounts to an average savings of $3,000 to $6,000 per year! Now that you know how to save thousands without using the scissors on the Sunday paper, remember to look for coupons and savings for printer ink and paper, the tradeoff for switching to Internet coupons, but one that will quickly pay for itself.

Buy in Bulk

Purchasing nonperishable items in bulk online, by phone, or from a warehouse store can save a great deal of money. Also consider automatic monthly delivery for health and personal care products. Auto delivery ensures products won't run out and shipping is often free. This type of bulk buying is different than the previous example, where the store suggests you'll save if you buy five containers of Morton Salt! Buying bulk online or at BJs and other member shopping clubs keep you in control over which products you can safely assume you'll need to replace more often.

Shop Senior Discounts

According to "theseniorlist.com," an excellent resource for savings and reviews, there are about 100 restaurants, retail, and grocery store chains that offer senior discounts, and some are quite generous. To name just a few, seniors are entitled to:

- *15% off at Belk on the first Tuesday of each month*
- *20% off at Rite Aid on the first Wednesday of each month*
- *10% off at Chick-Fil-A, or a free drink or coffee*
- *10% off at Wendy's*
- *5% off at Kroger one day per week*

Finally, keep in mind that this just refers to the discounts offered by large chains. Thousands of local and regional businesses offer senior discounts as well. Many are offered to people as young as 55. So, whether or not you consider yourself to be a "senior citizen" just yet, those 10% and 15% discounts can add up to hundreds or even thousands in savings each year.

Financial and Tax Advice

Your home is likely your greatest asset. With home loan rates at 50-year lows, take a careful look at refinancing. How much will it cost you? Divide this by the number of years you expect to stay in your home. Then look at how much your monthly payments would decline with a lower mortgage rate. How many years will it take for you to come out ahead? If it is only a few years, get yourself into a bank or other mortgage lender now.

If your home is about paid off and you are living expenses are greater than your income. Consider a reverse mortgage. These pay you monthly checks that do not need to be repaid. However, do not even consider talking to a bank or broker without discussing any program affecting your assets especially your home and any retirement funds! The bank or broker makes money by selling you their products, so be sure you get advice from a trusted professional not affiliated with your questions.

Consider Home Care

According to a 2010 consumer healthcare survey, the average annual rate for a private room in a nursing home is over $80,000! The annual cost in an assisted living community is over $40,000. Homecare can be half the cost, and often just 20-30 hours a week can mean the difference between living at home independently and needing to move to a facility.

Visiting Angels provides a cost-effective alternative. Caregivers provide assistance with meal preparation, light housekeeping, hygiene assistance, shopping, errands, and appointments, for a few hours a day to 24/7 care, in the comfort of home at affordable rates.

Adults want to retain their independence and maintain their own schedules. Skilled nursing facilities run their meal schedules, bathing and activities on a planned schedule, but with visiting Angels, the care recipient is in complete control of their own daily schedule.

Chapter 20- The Power of Pets

Debbie Waldecker

Unconditional love is often times the best medicine. Pets have been scientifically reported to lower stress levels and increase endorphins that promote physical, mental and emotional health benefits. Even though it may be difficult for some home bound seniors to care for a pet, the benefits may far exceed the risks.

Studies have shown that people who have pets also have lower blood pressure and cholesterol levels, which equate to a healthier heart. That loving feeling one gets when interacting with their pet is not just superficial and temporary. Heart attack risk is lessened by these factors, creating long lasting benefits. Seniors may also reap the heart healthy rewards of exercise when walking their dog or playing a game of fetch with "Fido".

Pets can provide motivation to get moving that often times, a family member or therapist just cannot. This simple act of moving can lead to a healthy heart, decreased obesity, speed up recovery for those who have suffered a heart attack, aid those undergoing physical therapy for an injury or stroke rehabilitation, stimulate blood flow in otherwise sedentary seniors that may be experiencing skin breakdown/pressure ulcers; and provide a diversion for those that may be lonely or suffering from grief or depression.

Stress is reduced with a cuddle! Patient recovery rates are improved when patients are with their pets. Exposure to our pets somehow elevates our serotonin and dopamine levels creating a calming, relaxing feeling; sometimes even creating a decreased need for pain or anxiety related medications. And so we dubbed the acronym-PETS—standing for Positive Emotional Trigger Stimulators. Pets have empathy for their humans. They sense sadness, loneliness, stress and a gamut of human emotions. They can alter their behavior to reflect their perceptions. Their mere presence is soothing. Imagine the soothing feeling of looking at an aquarium full of beautiful colorful tropical fish!

Pets can be just the ticket for giving their owners a sense of purpose. Purpose…. a reason to exist; what better reason than to love and be loved. Pets are the gentle, friendly solution for aging adults who may be in pain, depressed, grieving or lonely. We have seen patients whose lives revolve around caring for their pet... a family member whose grieving process is made easier by caring for the two Great Danes owned by her daughter who passed away and my own father who has diabetes and Alzheimer's Disease whose day is brightened when his pets come to visit him in the VA nursing home. Pets lift spirits and ease depression—decrease feelings of isolation and promote socialization. They are conversation starters and ice breakers when meeting someone new. Pets are also good providers of distraction, allowing us to refocus and perhaps temporarily forget an ache, a pain or sadness while in their presence.

Dogs can even detect disease. They are used as therapy pets because they have a keen sense of smell. This unique ability is because some breeds of dogs can pick up a smell more than 100,000 times better than a human. They can detect gases called Volatile Organic Compounds or VOC's making them great identifiers of diseases like epilepsy, diabetes and even cancer. Dogs have been trained to detect low blood sugar and warn their diabetic owners that they must take action. They can detect an upcoming epileptic seizure, (Bloomberg Business—
http://www.bloomberg.com/news/articles/2014-05-18/canines-cancer-sniffing-snouts-offer-new-testing-option) and are even being trained to detect prostate, ovarian and lung cancer.

Structure is very important to the elderly. Having a daily routine in place to care for a pet can aid in the regimen of self-care. This structure can be very important to seniors with memory loss who are more apt to remember the needs of their pets before their own needs. Care plans can be paired together for encouragement purposes. For example, regular meal schedules and exercise time. When paired together with pet care create more compliance. So often a senior's appetite is lowered for a number of medical reasons, but if meal time is scheduled at the same time as their pets; it can often create a stimulus for both the patient and pet to dine. Just a structured routine as simple as feeding the fish in the aquarium or taking the dog for a walk can help with keeping a loved one's interest in an activity and maintain focus.

Owning a pet can be made easier if the responsibility of providing pet care is left to the caregiver. "Forever" friends may be just what the doctor ordered. In fact, pet ownership is often times the ice breaker when a caregiver is introduced to a senior in need of home care. The furry family member is an instant subject of conversation even in the most difficult, hard to "get to know" patient. Pets become the common denominator.

Home care providers should always ask for pet names to include with initial assessments and caregivers should be selected based on their interaction with not only their patients, but with the patient's pet. Differences between patient and caregiver can become miniscule when a pet is in place to bridge the gap to a common ground. Reflection on past pets or stories about pets can surface fond memories of happy times. Pictures of pets, past and present, always stir up pleasantries in conversation when a patient/senior is having a difficult day.

For those that cannot have a pet, there are groups that provide "pet therapy". At our Agency, we occasionally bring our five pound shorkie, Zeus, in to see our clients who stop in to visit. Even our Alzheimer's patients will remember him and ask where he is on the days that Zeus is not there. The joy that our little dog brings to our clients is limitless and evident in the smiles and conversations that his mere presence conjures. Our little Zeus has definitely earned his "Angel wings"! Chocolate is the only consolation for one of our clients, when Zeus is not there to greet her.

There are many organizations that assist the elderly in finding an appropriate pet or providing "pet therapy". Some noteworthy organizations are Paws.org; Pet Partners and Pets for the Elderly. Pets for the Elderly is a charitable organization that helps seniors adopt pets from participating shelters by paying pet adoption fees. This program not only saves the life of an animal, but makes pet ownership possible. Local SPCA programs are always looking for volunteers to help feed and visit with their current adoptees and seniors with experience caring for pets that may not want any long term commitments may also look into the foster programs available. Other organizations look for senior volunteers to help other seniors in caring for their pets.

Sometimes laughter isn't the only best medicine. Scientific research has shown that elderly pet owners make fewer visits to their doctor than seniors without pets. That comforting feeling from a slimy doggie kiss, or the warm cuddles of a purring feline will work wonders over an apple a day to keep the doctor away!

Chapter 21- Seniors and Safety Issues
David Forman

Senior Safety: Preventing Illness and Accidents In And Out Of The Home

A home care aid has the primary responsibility of the safety of their care recipient while aiding with all the Activities of Daily Living (ADL's), but home care companies like Visiting Angels do far more to ensure safety and comfort to help seniors live independently.

During an initial assessment visit, an experienced employee will look for safety hazards and make suggestions that help prevent accidents. Some homes are already well equipped, but others may need a home makeover to help seniors "age in place."

Home Makeovers to Help Seniors 'Age in Place'

Nearly everyone hopes to "age-in-place," a term used by healthcare professionals to mean seniors remaining in their own homes, rather than moving to assisted living or otherwise having to move from their primary residence. As health conditions and needs change, it is not always a matter of simple choice, but a serious decision that necessitates discussions among entire families. Often times, changes to the home are required. In other words, the home must be "seniorized" for safety.

The following suggestions are timely for seniors returning from a hospital visit or a rehabilitation facility and all seniors and families who wish to prevent accidents and hospital readmissions.

1) **Safety first:**
   a. Fireproof your home.
      i. Always have a working fire extinguisher in your kitchen;
      ii. Install and check batteries in all smoke alarms;
      iii. Refrain from using candles and never leave them unattended;
      iv. Clean your lint trap with every dryer use; - Do not overload electrical wires;
   b. Install a carbon monoxide detector that sounds an alarm, close to bedrooms and living rooms;
   c. Update lighting throughout the home
      i. Use motion-detecting lighting;
      ii. Light all stairs, porches and entryways;
      iii. Use nightlights in bedrooms, baths and hallways;
   d. Establish an emergency escape plan in case of fire, storms, or other disasters;
   e. Keep at least five days' worth of bottled water and non-perishable foods available;
   f. Consider a Life-Alert-type system and wear it!

2) **Remove hazards around the home:**
   a. Build a small ramp over main doorway entrance thresholds;

b. Remove throw rugs, especially when transitioning to a cane, walker or wheelchair;

c. Repair loose carpet or raised areas of flooring;

3) **Make bathrooms safer:**
   a. Install grab handles in bathrooms;
   b. Place non-skid mats inside and outside your shower or tub and near the toilet and sinks;
   c. Use shower chairs and bath benches;
   d. Have your bathtub converted to a walk-in shower;

4) **Make daily activities simpler:**
   a. Store household items on lower shelves so that you can easily reach them;
   b. Use a reaching device that you can buy at any pharmacy or medical supply store;
   c. If you have trouble seeing, purchase a phone with larger numbers;
   d. If you have to climb for something, use a stepstool with handrails;
   e. Wear low-heeled, comfortable shoes that fit well and give your feet good support;
   f. Consider services that come to your home, such as in-home hairstyling.

These home makeover recommendations are an important first step to help seniors age in place. Home caregivers like our Angels help even more to prevent accidents and help people retain their independence.

Falls top the list of types of fatal in-home accidents for seniors

Falls are the single largest cause of injury among seniors and top the list of in-home accidental fatalities. The Center for Disease Control and Prevention's (CDC) National Center for Injury Prevention and Control, offers the following statistics:

"Older adults are hospitalized for fall-related injuries five times more often than they are for injuries from other causes. A third of older adults who fall sustain a hip fracture and are hospitalized, die within a year."

Even if a fall does not result in hospitalization, fear of falling can become a major factor in seniors' quality of life, as fear leads to inactivity and loss of confidence, which in turn produces a cycle of loss of self-confidence and greater inactivity. "Tripping and falling is nearly always preventable," said Annalise Forman, one of the owners of our Visiting Angels franchise. "As seniors, or caregivers to seniors, prevention should be a top priority."

"Medication side effects and drug interactions should be completely understood, and may require consistent monitoring and reminding," said Annalise Forman, co-owner of Visiting Angels in Southern Delaware. "The majority of medications for seniors may have some effect on alertness and, or blood pressure, which can lead to loss of balance. Ask both your physician and pharmacist!"

"Mobility and agility limitations also require a fresh look at the everyday contents of the home," she added, offering some tips to help minimize the risk of life-altering falls for loved ones:

- ➢ Understand medication side effects and interactions and post warnings clearly in your home where you keep your medicine.
- ➢ When adding or switching drugs, or adjusting dosage for the first time, keep physical activity to a minimum. It is better to wait an hour, watching television or reading a book, than sweeping or climbing stairs.
- ➢ Throw rugs can be a tripping hazard. Either remove them or make sure they are securely tacked down.
- ➢ Add hand-rails to all stairs.
- ➢ Clear clutter from walking paths and make sure hallways and stairways are well lit.
- ➢ Eliminate long extension cords that snake across a room. Plug lamps into outlets near the wall so cords are tucked away.
- ➢ Add grab bars next to the toilet, tub and shower.
- ➢ Getting in and out of the tub can be hazardous. In addition to grab bars, make sure the tub has non-skid mats. A tub seat may make showering easier, too.
- ➢ Trade in floppy slippers for well-fitting slippers with non-skid soles.
- ➢ Avoid night clothing that drags on the ground.

Seniors' in-home accidents are often balance-related

Many people do not think they are that at risk of falling simply because they have never fallen, or because they do not feel imbalanced. Unfortunately, by the time you can tell you may have a problem the problem has already become severe.

There very simple, non-invasive tests that your doctor can use to assess your fall risk. A "Get Up and Go" test takes about 20 seconds. You'll be observed as you rise from a straight back chair, walk 10 feet and return to the chair. If you already use a cane or walker, the results are assessed the same.

Other tests involve performing basic tasks used to rate your ability to maintain balance while performing normal activities of daily living at home.

Many people who believe they will easily pass these tests find that they are at greater risk than they thought and can then take preventative measures, such as removing common hazards throughout the home or installing grab bars in the bathroom.

As we age, we lose bone density and muscle tone and we may be taking medications that affect blood pressure – all common contributors to injury producing accidents. It is important to discuss with your doctor how these factors affect you, because fall statistics are alarming:

- ➢ More than one in three people 65 or older fall each year and the risk of falling rises proportionally with age.
- ➢ Falls are the No. 1 cause of fractures, hospital admissions for trauma and accidental-injury deaths.
- ➢ Two-thirds of those who experience a fall will fall again within six months.
- ➢ Often fall-related fractures are at the arm, hand, ankle, spine, pelvis or hip – any of which may cause a loss of independence for a long period of time.

Depending on the injury, most hospitals and rehabilitation facilities will not discharge a patient unless they can be assured that there is continued care coverage at home. Since falls are unexpected, families are usually not prepared to provide the total amount of time needed to care for their loved one.

Annalise offers further encouragement for families. "To a person recovering from an injury, their biggest concerns are about becoming a burden to family and losing their independence. Visiting Angels addresses both of these fears. We often meet with a care recipient and the family while the care recipient is still recovering in a facility, so that when ready to return home, there will be a friendly, familiar face ready to help."

"Most people develop a fear of falling that increases with age," added Annalise, "For those with a previous fall history, this fear can become debilitating, and many will avoid very basic activities of daily living and adopt a more sedentary lifestyle, which can rapidly lead to more serious health problems."

"Many of our clients who began to use our services because of an injury retain our services long after their recovery. They find that just a little extra help makes a huge difference in their ability to remain independent and enjoy a better quality of life," Annalise concludes.

Speak with your doctor about your balance and risk of falling. Do a home inspection. Observe your loved ones closely! It all matters and it all makes them safer and gives you a greater peace of mind!

Chapter 22- Battling Depression and Anxiety with Compassion
David Forman

Home Care "Angels" Offer Seniors Hope

Media reports, often placed by the publicity firms of pharmaceutical companies, would have you believe there's an epidemic of both clinical depression and anxiety disorders among virtually every population from children and teens, to adults and seniors. There's no denying that the number of people suffering from depression is large and spans all ages. However, too many people with quite normal sadness brought on by grief, loneliness, or other situational issues are treated as if they have a permanent chemical imbalance.

It is important to distinguish between a normal short-term response to stress and life-altering issues and situations. Realistic concern about physical problems and illness, serious life circumstances, and prescription medications all make it difficult to separate a normal level of anxiety or adverse symptoms (side effects) of medication, from a treatable issue or long-term disorder. Regardless of short-term situation, or longer-term brain chemistry, there's no need for any individual to suffer needlessly.

Unfortunately, many people have the false belief that anxiety lessens with age. The truth is that many older adults with an anxiety disorder had one when they were younger, and others develop life-affecting anxiety from the stresses they face. These stresses might be from chronic illness, changing conditions, cognitive impairment and of course depression from significant emotional losses.

According to Healthyplace.com, a Web site devoted to mental health, nearly half of those with clinical depression also meet the criteria for anxiety disorder, and about a quarter of those diagnosed with anxiety disorder also suffer depression. Although anti-depressant and anti-anxiety medications can make you feel better regardless of the cause, there are healthier alternatives that both address emotional wellbeing and help provide a much better overall quality of life.

There's an important difference between simply living without anxiety and depression vs. actually living with some degree of happiness, interest and joy. From visiting thousands of care recipients and their families, we find the vast majority of seniors suffering from depression are those living alone. Companionship, for even a few hours a day, can be as effective as anti-depressant medications in helping someone through and beyond any period of pain and suffering. Having connections to people who somebody is looking forward to see again, provides a healthy dose of anticipation, hope and connectedness. The consequences are an increasing self-worth and the will to live and enjoy life better at any stage.

While there's nothing wrong with the use of anti-anxiety and anti-depressant medications for shorter-term treatment during periods of grief, adding additional medication to a daily regimen of other medications is clearly not the best long-term solution. Medications can mask our anxiety and pain, but they can't create new opportunities for a happier existence. Relationships with other people can, and do.

The companionship that our "Angels" provide adds to a person's joy in life. Just a few hours a day, or even a few hours a week, can make all the difference to somebody living alone, especially those who had a spouse or other companions throughout their lives.

When a person is suffering, he or she is usually not caring for themselves and their homes. They're not eating regularly or right, they're not cleaning the bathrooms or doing dishes, making meals or running the laundry, and they're especially not getting out and about away from home. For many, especially women, a messy house and poor diet are like wearing heavy anchor weights while trying to climb out from the hole of depression, it is not long before the person suffering all but gives up. These periods also make a person ripe for catching a host of stress-related illnesses.

Experienced caregivers normally recognize symptoms of depression and can alert family members so that it can be properly addressed.

Angels help with all normal activities of daily living such as personal care, light housekeeping, meal preparation, errands and transportation, and provide respite for family caregivers. All these normal activities are especially important during times of great stress or depression. Too many people are truly suffering unnecessarily, when identifying the problem and a bit of companionship can make a world of difference. Nobody should have to face depression alone.

Studies confirm the common sense notion that loneliness significantly raises the risk of loss of physical functioning and earlier-than-expected death. The *New York Times* recently published the details of a report from the *Archives of Internal Medicine* that showed that over a period of six years, nearly 25 percent of seniors feeling isolated and lonely, experience a significant decline in their ability to perform activities of daily living; to bathe, dress, eat, toilet and get up from a chair or a bed on their own. Lonely older adults also were 45 percent more likely to die within this period than those who felt meaningfully connected with others.

Andrew Steptoe, director of the Institute of Epidemiology and Health Care at University College, London, has been studying this subject and said, "There is growing evidence that both loneliness and social isolation are related to biological processes that may increase health risk, including changes in immune and inflammatory processes and disruption of stress-related hormones." Another study from Cornell University on the physiological effects of loneliness showed that the blood pressure of older people rises in reaction to some kinds of stress and that loneliness accentuates this response.

This is why Visiting Angels caregivers are chosen not only for their experience and skills, but also for their compassion and kindness. We listen to families' needs and preferences and do our best to pair personality types properly. The personal connection between our "Angels" and our clients is just as important as the personal services they provide. Over time some pairings grow and thrive, and others for one reason or another do not seem to click. That's to be expected occasionally, but a new experienced and competent friendly face is usually just a phone call away.

Recognizing and Treating Anxiety and Depression in Seniors

Your family physician can also order a short-term course of anti-anxiety medication. However, be aware that long-term use of short-acting anti-anxiety medications may eventually add to depression.

Sudden or unexplained anxiety or depression without a cause is very likely a result of prescription medication, over-the-counter products or a combination of both. E-MEDTV.com, a health information Web site written by medical experts, lists worsening depression as the side effect of many of these short-acting anti-anxiety medications. Some common culprits: *Xanax, Ativan* or other short-acting anti-anxiety medications (usually benzodiazepines) are great for "as needed" situations but should not be used as a sleep aid unless the cause of insomnia is anxiety. After just a few consecutive days of use of these drugs when used exclusively for sleep, people report a "feeling of doom" or similar symptoms of depression. Speak to your doctor about how to use these meds only as necessary.

Since anxiety and depression are caused by chemical imbalances, the chemistry of medication is going to be the No. 1 culprit. Medication-induced anxiety or depression can be caused by incorrect dosing or drug interactions, or may simply be your body's normal response to a particular medication. While your doctor or pharmacist can tell you what side affects you may experience, remember that their information is based on studies of a whole lot of people that aren't you. That folded paper disclaimer that's required of the drug companies to list all side effects, tells you that taking their medicine can cause everything from seizures to diarrhea. Try not to over react from reading the side effect lists until after you think you may be experiencing any, or you may just find yourself experiencing seizures on the toilet just from reading the suggestion!

Similarly, nighttime pain meds, such as Tylenol PM or Advil PM, when used just for the purpose of helping you get to sleep, are notorious for causing morning depression, irritability and even confusion the following day. Long-term use causes kidney damage. Ask your doctor about nighttime sleep aids that are designed specifically for sleep, or try sublingual melatonin, which is available at any drug store. Our bodies produce melatonin as our sleep regulator, making it generally safe and naturally effective.

"While your doctor or pharmacist can tell you what side affects you may experience, remember that their information is based on studies of lots of people that aren't you!"

Several of today's anti-depressant medications also effectively treat general anxiety disorder and can truly raise a person's quality of life — helping, rather than worsening, these symptoms. When reviewing your medication routine, your goal should be to reduce the overall number of different meds and be 100 percent sure that your remaining medication's dosage is correct for your personal needs.

It is also important to note that medical conditions and prescription medications can be a cause of depression. According to helpguide.org, an online health and lifestyle resource, an illness may have depression as a symptom or be a psychological reaction to a chronic condition especially if it is painful, disabling or terminal; and several medications list anxiety/restlessness and worsening depression as clinically significant side effects.

Illnesses causing depression include:
Parkinson's, stroke, heart disease, cancer, diabetes, thyroid disorders, vitamin deficiencies, Alzheimer's, lupus, multiple sclerosis, chronic pain, and especially illnesses with less well-known prognosis.

Medications that can cause or worsen depression include:
- Blood pressure meds
- Beta-blockers
- Sleeping pills, including PM pain meds like AdvilPM or TylenolPM when used long term
- Anxiety meds (i.e. Valium, Xanax, Halcion)
- Calcium-channel blockers
- Medication for Parkinson's disease
- Ulcer medication (e.g. Zantac, Tagamet)
- Heart drugs containing reserpine
- Steroids (e.g. cortisone and prednisone)
- High-cholesterol drugs (e.g. Lipitor, Mevacor, Zocor)
- Painkillers and arthritis drugs
- Estrogens (e.g. Premarin, Prempro)

If you feel depressed after starting any new medication, talk to your doctor. You may be able to lower your dose or switch to another medication that doesn't impact your mood.

Many common illnesses, such as dementia and Parkinson's, create symptoms such as agitation that mimic anxiety. Some medications and their interactions or incorrect dosing can cause changes in breathing and heart rate that can also be mistaken for anxiety. Similarly, some illnesses, such as a stroke, may cause personality changes that may seem like either anxiety or depression, and medications of virtually every type also may cause depression. With so many possible causes of anxiety and depression, where do you start to look for solutions? While diagnosis and treatment in most cases should start with the primary-care physician, individuals or their loved ones can consider the following first:

Life Circumstances

The loss of a life-long partner, spouse, family member or friend brings with it a normal process of grief. Situational depression is a horrible part of life as a human being. The same brain dealing with loss or other mentally "depressing" situations is also the control center for the body's physical responses. Situational depression and anxiety is completely normal. This does not mean that you shouldn't see your doctor. In fact, examinations done close to these times of stress may bring otherwise difficult diagnostic issues to light.

Grief

Grief Share meetings and spiritual counseling is available at most houses of worship throughout Sussex County, as well as around the country. If you haven't been active in a church or synagogue, now may be the time God is calling you to join with a body of believers to minister to your needs. With a 100% mortality rate, most of us give more thought to what's next when we see our friends are already on their way to finding out.

My wife Annalise and I moved to Southern Delaware from the NYC metro area, leaving careers with six-figure salaries to open Visiting Angels, thinking it as mission work, more than a job or investment. The goal was to help as many families as possible, and we make no attempt to hide our Christian values and background. We certainly do not discriminate or even ask our caregiver applicants about their religious beliefs.

However, many Christians, both employees and care recipient families are drawn to the Visiting Angels name, and we have been blessed to find Southern Delaware has a population of believers strong in the faith. Many care recipients have been thrilled to learn of our mission goals and about our faith, and have asked if our "Angels" would read their Bible to them, take them to Church on Sundays, or sing along to pianos or recorded music at home. Hospice patients, or those expressing a strong preference have been open to discussing their faith, and our Angels are trained to listen and offer hope in these cases. Generally, with homecare like most businesses, politics and religion are nearly always off-limit subjects. You and your family may feel very differently, and that preference is given as much respect if not more when necessary. However, your feelings about your faith should be brought up during an initial meeting with a Director or owner, and may play a part in matching like-minded pairs.

Nobody should have to face anxiety or depression alone. From a few hours a week, to 24/7 care, Visiting Angels compassionate caregivers can help. Call 877-583-8715 or go to visitingangels.com

Chapter 23- Benefits of Music in Homecare
Debra Desrosiers

"Music can lift us out of depression or move us to tears. It is a remedy, a tonic, orange juice for the ear. But for many of my neurological patients, music is even more. It can provide access, even when no medication can, to movement, to speech, to life. For them, music is not a luxury, but a necessity." Oliver Sacks, Neurologist and Author, 1933 – 2015

If I had to pick one single activity that has the ability to instantly sooth, motivate, redirect, engage anybody in a unique and personal way, I would put money on music. Music, when used strategically, can be used in homecare to affect behaviors using a person-centered approach.

While giving an in-service to our staff ending a section on music I had asked if anyone would like to share any experiences with the group. Angela shared her experience by explaining a case she recently was assigned inside an assisted living facility. Our agency was brought in for an end of life case for Jim. Jim needed one to one care to keep him safe. Angela was providing services in the overnight hours and Jim was ánxious and could not sleep. Angela explained that the care plan read Jim was Catholic so she used her I-Phone to google Catholic hymns. Angela began to play

some hymns on her phone. Angela shared that soon after she started to play them Jim looked over and said, "Thank you". Jim then drifted off to sleep. Angela told the group how amazed and transformed Jim was from this simple task of playing music. Jaws dropped in the meeting and we all learned the importance of music and bring this lesson to our homes on a daily basis to help others. The following account of Al and Martha illustrates another story of how music is a go-to solution.

One of our case managers and I were doing a routine home visit. As we entered a cute little home in Manchester, NH owned by clients Al and Martha, we were about to witness a miraculous display of the immediate and useful power of music. Al had mid-stage Alzheimer's disease. He was a tall man with an aggressive demeanor. His wife of over 50 years, Martha, had arranged for homecare services to give her a little, much needed, respite.

Martha was a tiny, well-dressed and soft spoken woman. She was doing her best to keep it together. Al's caregiver was expected any minute but had not arrived yet. The scene seemed surreal as Al was literally in Martha's face while she was trying to wrap up a conversation on the phone. His tone of voice sounded intimidating, yet his words were jumbled together in a way that did not create understandable sentences, at least to me.

Al was in his eighties. If someone who did not speak English was listening to him, they would probably think he was perfectly fine based on his confident tone of voice and clear body gestures. Martha was at her wit is end and was looking for some way to pacify the intensity of her husband's mood in the moment.

There we all were in the kitchen: our case manager, me, Al, and Martha. All eyes were on Al whose tone of voice was escalating. He appeared to be on the verge of exploding at his wife over something, but no one knew what it was. There she was, trying not to crumble.

Our case manager was highly skilled in working with someone with Alzheimer's disease. She redirected Al into the living room, leaving Martha and I in the kitchen for a moment. As he left the room, Martha started taking big breaths trying to calm herself down.

As our case manager did her best to negotiate and check in with Al, he did his best to dominate the conversation with sentences that never ended and, again, were jumbled words. His tone of voice seemed to match a totally coherent dialogue. At that moment, Al's caregiver, Sheila, arrived and Martha slipped out of the house.

Sheila breezed into the living room, quickly sized up the situation, and went right to work, so to speak. She went right up to him, got down to his level, and with a big smile let him know who she was (even though he had been her client for some time) and told him she was happy to see him. Still, Al continued to speak in a loud and aggressive tone.

Sheila made a bee-line over to the stereo and let the music Al loved do the heavy lifting. The switch was flipped and the scene instantly shifted as Sheila put on one of Al's favorite albums. As soon as the first few notes floated across the room into Al's ears and landed in his limbic system, Al jumped up from his chair, started snapping his fingers, and broke into a huge smile. Al stood right in front of Sheila and started to dance. She matched him and started to dance with him while casually talking to him. She was prepping him for the day. Everything had transformed literally within seconds. No drugs, no restraints, no threats. Only a man listening to music he had enjoyed when he was at the prime of his life with a caregiver who knew how to use music to create a moment of joy which was also helping her do her job.

The instant transformation of Al was remarkable and a testament to the power of music. It was an inspiring scene to witness. For caregivers handling challenging behaviors with clients or patients, well-chosen person-centered music is a valuable tool in their care-giving toolbox.

Using Music in Homecare: A Person-Centered Approach
The benefits of music in homecare is a broad topic but here are some guidelines to get started. Keep an open mind (and ears and eyes) and stay flexible. Timing and approach are important factors to consider when setting up this new ingredient as an intentional part of a care plan. Most importantly, when choosing music for your client, use a person-centered approach.

Start with a core playlist of the music they listened to when they were a teenager and young adult. Who were their favorite musicians? Which songs by those musicians were their favorites? This can take some research and gentle questioning, but if you can find at least a couple good tunes to start with, it is likely that as you play the songs, the music will activate memories for your client. They may be able to provide a list of songs for you directly.

A new program sweeping the US is the "Music and Memory" program. This groundbreaking program was created by retired social worker Dan Cohen.

See www.musicandmemory.org. Music and Memory brings personalized music into the lives of the elderly or infirmed through digital music technology. Who can take this training and use this program? Nursing home staff, elder care professionals, as well as family caregivers, can learn how to create personalized playlists using iPods or other audio players. For those working with individuals who are struggling with Alzheimer's, dementia, and other cognitive challenges, this program provides an approach worth its weight in gold.

If you haven't seen the documentary on the program *Alive Inside* you will be astounded at the accounts and possibilities of this program when done well. In a homecare setting, the headphones would not be necessary. However, in a residential facility, each resident uses headphones so as not to dominate the soundscape of the environment.

We talked with Joshua Freitas, Reflections & Engagement Manager at LCB Senior Living and author of *The Dementia Concept*. Josh holds five certifications related to dementia care and has studied at some of the world's most renowned colleges and universities including Lesley University, Harvard University, and Berklee College of Music. One of the chapters in his books is "Music as Medicine" in which he describes a 6-month experiment with 35 residents in a memory care facility who suffered from the symptoms of sundown syndrome.

Josh writes, "The Music as Medicine model involves choosing appropriate music to be played for the group during different times of the day. In our experiment, the Music as Medicine model resulted in a decrease of the number of participants who experienced sun downing, reducing the number from 35 to 9 people. You can recreate this project by playing music in the living environment every day and paying special attention to three unique stages of the day which dictate the kind of music to play."

Josh outlines three stages of the day and recommends what type of music is recommended for each stage. It is worth repeating that when choosing which music to play, it is very important to take into account the individual preference, age, and ethnicity of the listener.

Stage 1

This takes place in the morning. The guideline is upbeat, popular, instrumental music with a melody to which participants can sing along. Joshua generously permits us to include the following passage from his book.

"Engaging with music increases serotonin and causes feelings of happiness and well-being. The morning, Stage 1, is an important stage of the day because it sets the tone for the rest of the day. The morning is like the first domino that is pushed over onto a long line of standing dominoes, each falling in turn. A successful start causes a ripple effect which results in better mood and behavior throughout the day. By playing this kind of music, the music that they listened to primarily between the ages of 18-25, it promotes a familiar and safe environment.

Stage 2

"This starts late morning or lunch time. Upbeat but not well-known instrumental music is recommended. This type of music creates a "pleasant background noise that allows the brain to benefit from an increased production of serotonin but does not detract from social engagement. [It] increases a sense of ease in the body but does not over-stimulate or distract the mind from activities, conversation, or attentiveness to eating at mealtimes. Music with lyrics ... is not recommended at mealtimes because lyrics and lyrical melodies may encourage people to sing along while eating, which can cause choking.

Stage 3

"This cycle takes place in the evenings when the sun is setting. Music recommended here is music with one line of melody, which causes the brain to release dopamine which replaces the mind and body. The evening [the choice of music] is best suited for those mindless but necessary tasks of daily life, such as sorting and folding laundry." The outcome of this experiment yielded a marked decrease in choking and the sun downing behaviors of the thirty-five residents were reduced to nine residents.

We thank and acknowledge Josh for allowing us to share the above information from his book into this chapter in efforts to help families choose music wisely and effectively as a part of a care plan.

In a one-to-one setting, working with a client to develop a list of their favorite songs would be an activity all by itself. This activity alone would prompt numerous walks down memory lane. Another activity along the same line, is surfing on YouTube for the client's favorite songs. This requires that the client has high speed internet or the caregiver has a smart phone or tablet they are willing to use.

Here are several accounts submitted from caregivers at our Auburn, NH agency on their experience with Music in Homecare.

From Caregiver Susan

"Music is a strong force in my client's care. When I arrive and find he is agitated, irritated, or out of sorts, I will first sit quietly and listen to him about his day. He loves to watch golf, but I know he loves his classical country music so I will often suggest he flip the channel to his favorite music. He immediately will respond how he can read and listen to that music. He also tells me this music relaxes him. Once he is relaxed, we can address the core issue he is experiencing. Often times he will retire at 8:30 in the evening, unless we are deep into a conversation (music in the background), and I will leave the music on for him for 15-20 minutes."

From Caregiver Donna

"I recently provided service to a woman who is difficult. I transport her and intentionally play very calming instrumental music on the car stereo. She told me she had gone to Woodstock in the '60s and much preferred Jimi Hendrix, Grateful Dead, and Led Zeppelin. I use music to calm myself and I can't imagine getting a warm fuzzy from those performers, at least at this time in my life. . When I go to support my CA patients and even engage in hospice, I typically have some wonderful Christian music that soothes and calms them. If they are from my own parish, I know their likes and select music from Steubenville. If they are from another parish, I will typically bring traditional music such as John Michael Talbot or the safety net of David Lanz. Music is a great source for healing and calming.

From Caregiver Chris

"I have a station of classical music programed on my car radio so that whenever I am driving one of my clients we have that soothing music to listen to and we both 'enjoy' the ride all the more."

From Caregiver Nancy

"My client was very agitated and couldn't sit still, so I put on some Elvis music. He liked it and he quieted right down. He even went to sleep for a while. Later the daughter-in-law came back to check on him and he woke up. It was the end of my shift so I left and the next day I got a call letting me know he passed during the night."

From Caregiver Louisa

"My client, Joanie, has mid-stage Parkinson's. We sat next to each other and got onto the internet. We went to YouTube and pulled up one of her favorites songs. She was totally captivated with these videos. She was so excited; just like she was transported back in time seeing the songs performed live! It was the highlight of her day. We kept looking up songs and the stories she told me were priceless. YouTube is a great resource for finding music from years past and enjoying them with my clients."

From Caregiver Giselle

Giselle created a great double activity using both favorite music and Google searches. Giselle's client, Harry, is 97 years old. Harry is the poster child for a home care success story. Harry was once a high-powered corporate executive. After an accident in his late 80s, he was confined to a wheelchair and placed in a nursing home. Harry was very unhappy in a facility and decided to return home and hire non-medical home care services to take care of him. Harry loved music and although he was frequently hallucinating, could still connect well with music he enjoyed as a young man. One of his caregivers, Giselle, keyed in to Harry's love of music right away. It began with Harry's desire to sing a Frank Sinatra tune. Harry was having trouble remembering the lyrics so Giselle googled the song's lyrics and in less than a minute, they were singing the song together.

Giselle shares, "I loved listening to him sing and now we could get through the whole song without a hiccup. I started singing with him which he loved as well." After singing, the conversation began about Frank Sinatra. Harry and I had a giggle when we tried to remember how many wives Frank had. Then we googled it! That led to another conversation that led to another. All from just one song." Giselle continued, "The music brings him back in time, back to that moment. It is so much fun! You never know where that song is going to take them. Once, Harry was musically transported to a Broadway play he attended with his wife in New York City many years ago. He told me all about that event and so many memories were triggered just by hearing that song. I feel so grateful to witness him enjoying the music and being there for him so he could tell his stories."

With a smart phone in hand, able to access music and the internet, caregivers have a world of activities at their fingertips! Giselle has several clients and talks to all of them about what kind of music they enjoy. She found an app in which you type in a birthday and year to find out what the #1 song was on that day.

And last, a special story from Caregiver Ashley

Victor Hugo (author of Les Misérables), a famous poet, playwright, and novelist, once said, "Music expresses that which cannot be put into words and that which cannot remain silent". This quotation proves to be very true, especially in home health care. Even though my experiences in healthcare have been few, there is one fact that I know to be true: music is the sound of the soul speaking.

All too often I have cared for clients who have lost their sight, speech, and/or cognitive abilities, such as memory, due to stroke, dementia, Alzheimer's, or another malady to the brain or body. However, one commonality between these individuals is their love of music. For Harry, who is often aggressive and paranoid, music soothes and calms him instantly (and he is happy to sing for hours). Whereas, Theresa is transported back to her parents' parlor where she would dance to big bands records and "feel unconditional love". While Virginia knows every word to all the "old" tunes because they were "World War II songs featured in a famous movie *South Pacific*".

Not only is music good for the soul, but it is also a universal language. "Momma", who does not speak English, and "Mom", who speaks broken English, both smile, clap, and even dance around when music is played; although they may not know the words, they feel the emotion of the singer's croon and the beat of the bass. They are ignited with a primal instinct to move, groove, and "shake it".

Even those who are unable to communicate verbally or physically can emotionally connect to music. Alice, who is wheelchair bound, unable to speak, and known to have frequent violent outbursts, was often thought to be an empty shell. However, when you looked into Alice's eyes, you could see her soul. From the moment we met, I knew I could find a way to get her involved in daily activities once again. Although I do not have a degree in Music Therapy or Gerontology, I was determined. Within a very short time, I found out that Alice enjoyed being outside and going for long walks. She could feel the warmth of the sun or her face and she loved to listen to the birds singing. One day while we were sitting together, I played one of her old records and she began to cry. I immediately reached for the needle to stop the song, but Alice touched my hand. She pointed to the smiley face (I had developed a system of pictures to help us communicate). From that moment on, I knew I had found the key to motivate, inspire and communicate with Alice more deeply than words or pictures would ever allow me to do.

These personal experiences with music in home healthcare and my own love of music, continue to encourage me to use music therapeutically in all of the work that I do. I hope this chapter has inspired thoughts of how music can be incorporated into a great care plan for your homecare clients. Remember to keep the main focus on a person-centered approach. Following the guidelines suggested in this chapter along with your own intuition, music can be a powerful tool in your caregiver toolbox.

Chapter 24- Long Distance Family Care
David Milby

"I got the Job!"
"We are getting Married!"
"The Deployment is only for a year!"

Whatever the circumstance may be for a "long distance family", everyone is heavily affected. Family dynamics are usually one thing that can make everyone crazy now and again but, when we add in a gaining concern for mom or dad's health or safety, we've got an even greater and more emotional puzzle to solve. We all want to help and we want things done right, but it is impossible to be in two places at once. The goal here must be to gain a true picture of what is needed and find the best possible way to fill the needs.

After helping and listening to thousands of clients and families over the years we have become experts at pulling in the right resources, strategizing communication options, connecting the dots and guiding the hard decisions. I have personally moved many times and have always had family in multiple states. I am also married to a Canadian and we work to keep up with her family across the border. Staying connected does take time and money, but when you've invested in the people you love nothing else could mean more.

The transition to caring for our parents is a weighted scale of strength and weakness. At one point all of our weaknesses as children needed the strength of our parents, but at a certain point (we hope) children gain strength and the load evens out. Gradually though as time moves on we begin to see some weakness creep up on our parents and this is where our strengths will be relied on.

Our first thoughts initially can be quite overwhelming. Where are mom and dad financially, mentally and physically? Are they telling me the full story? Should I move home or move mom or dad in with me? Who can I trust to help us? How much will this all cost? What about insurance, paperwork and the house? These are all questions we ask ourselves, but now is the time to get answers, make a plan and start acting. Planning and peace of mind are always worth the effort when it comes to our loved one's care, health and safety. Here's what we suggest as our "insider tips".

Building a Care Network

When we are not physically able to be there, the next best thing is to partner with someone who is. This may mean you need to call your brother, sister or other family member who is local and have a serious talk, but not everyone has the luxury of having a local confidant. In every aspect of senior care there are compassionate and professional people who can lead you in the right direction.

In our area where we serve we have gotten to know everyone from the local pharmacists, Doctors and specialists to the Firemen, Elder Law attorneys and Banking officers. It is not a nice thought to believe that your mom or dad might be hiding things from you or being taken advantage of, but it happens every day.

Many times we will get that first call from a son or daughter who is out of state and they will describe the family situation for us: "Mom and Dad are physically doing fine, but I think mom is starting to have some memory issues and dad is not wanting to do his exercising. I think it would be good to have someone come in and check on them once a week." We go to visit mom and dad and can see that dad's car is in bad shape from his driving with poor vision and he can barely get out of his chair, mom is more than slightly confused and is trembling with weakening muscles.

If it has been a while since you've actually been there, it can be hard to really know the full story. If you can, spend the time to visit with them, and develop a plan to build your care network. Find out when the next doctor's appointment is and ask if you can be there to meet or re-acquaintance yourself to their doctor. When you are at the doctors' office ask them who they recommend for services like Home Health, Hospice Care, Home Care and Physical Therapists. Also, make a note of mom and dad's prescriptions and check to see that they are all from the same pharmacist or doctor, check that all the prescriptions are on the medication list that they carry with them. When building a care network start researching and calling for information before the care is needed if possible. Ask about programs and services, cost, veterans programs and health insurance and keep a file to reference.

For all of the non-medical information, we need to find out who mom and dad are still close with and make a point to reach out to those individuals such as neighbors, friends, pastors, bankers, even the dry cleaner or lawn maintenance man. Make a trip to the bank with your parents and sit down with a banking officer to ask a few questions and do not forget to leave them your information. Have open and honest discussions about planning ahead and letting them know that you really care. If you end up getting resistance or they are in denial about needing help from their children (who might still be 12 years old in their mind), try planning a birthday party or anniversary party in their honor and invite as many guests as you can including everyone on the care network list you've created, another less expensive option is to get someone like their doctor or pastor to sit down with them and explain that it is time to start planning for the future and allowing others to lift the load. This advice from an "expert" is quite useful and it shifts the blame from the family members.

Communication Strategy

Now, we know that the vast majority of seniors needing care do not e-mail, text, FaceTime or Skype. Some do, but from my experience it is a very small percentage. Communicating with our parents isn't all that we are talking about here in this section, it is very important, but there is so much more.

Once we have built and established a care network than the next thing to do is work on your network communication. There are many advancements that are available right now to families that are not widely discussed. Here are a few examples that may open up communication:

- ➤ doctors are using patient portals for records and open communication with patients,
- ➤ sleep apnea machines can be monitored online for families to see oxygen levels,
- ➤ security camera video feed (Nanny Cams) can be viewed on

your smart phone 24/7,

- ➢ Home Care agencies (that are tech savvy) like ours let families and clients log on to view schedules, caregiver profiles, photos, and client care plans.
- ➢ Home goods and care supplies can be ordered and delivered via Amazon, Walmart, and Target can even be sent automatically every month.
- ➢ Banking accounts and credit cards can be accessed and monitored online plus you can add alert systems like Life-lock to protect from identity theft.
- ➢ Prescriptions can be ordered online and delivered to the home.
- ➢ Build your online calendar to share with other family members complete with appointment reminders and reminders to re-assess the main concerns every 3-6 months.
- ➢ Use an online cloud file sharing system such as iCloud Docs, Google Docs or Dropbox in order to be able to share or access important information from wherever you are.

Gone are the days where you have to go through the mail or call the doctor or wait for answers. We recommend systemizing your plan and building time into your schedule. Not only will you stay on top of things, but you will feel less anxious if you set aside a few hours each week or month to manage everything. As you are getting "down to business" remember to also schedule and remind yourself that it is always more than just a to do list or check system. Enjoy each moment of caring for your parent(s), start every call off with a fun story or joke, send pictures of the kids or pets and remember to communicate your love and appreciation for them.

All in all, we are suggesting that you begin to share information and gather the facts as early as possible. You wouldn't rely on just a phone call with your kids in college to make sure they are ok, you are checking accounts, Facebook, online grades and any other way you can gain information. Do the same thing for your parents, just because they say that they are doing fine and have nothing to complain about does not mean that everything is hunky dory. The same can be true for the opposite situation where mom or dad is always complaining or worried and, in fact, everything is actually totally under control.

The Move

Well, as time goes by and travelers get weary most families are ready to make some kind of move either back to or away from the homestead or somewhere in between. It may seem like you are mentally playing a game of human chess trying to figure out the right solution, but after enough contemplation, invested time and prayer the decision usually becomes clear. Right here we can outline a gradual line of care that you can follow minded that each individual case allows for exceptions.

1) **Right size living conditions-** Large estates, even large apartments can seem like an overwhelming amount of space to handle. When we conserve energy by caring for a smaller garden, or cleaning a smaller kitchen we feel much better at the end of the day. We also want to be very conscious of safety (think fall prevention & security)

2) **Schedule Partial Home Care & Push for Home Health as needed-** For the record, Home Care (such as Visiting Angels) is non-medical care and can be scheduled per the family as needed. Home Health is skilled medical care and is subject to insurance, Medicaid guidelines and doctor's orders (prescriptions).

3) **Rehabs and Physical Therapy-** After a general three-day hospital stay with pending conditions or after a surgery it is always wise to consider a short term rehab stay. Rehabs all around the country are building and renovating to have a relaxing and "spa" like feel. If an actual "stay" is not needed you can opt for outpatient therapy, but individuals must be both able to drive or find transportation and be motivated to continue exercise at home.

4) **Live in Care-** This type of care is needed when assistance is needed both day and night, with daily watchful oversight. You do have some hard choices here such as; 24/7 Home Care with a Certified Nursing Aid avoiding transition trauma and keeping to an already social agenda, an Assisted Living Community with a Registered Nurse onsite nurturing social activities, personally moving in with your parent(s) or having your parent(s) move in with you.

5) **Skilled Nursing Facility (Nursing Home)-** This is when your loved ones are in need of skilled medical care on a daily basis, where the family is unable to handle the need or care level.

6) **Hospice & Palliative Care-** Yes, I said the "H word", but Hospice care can come in and help when a serious diagnosis is made. We have heard of many beautiful stories of wishes coming true, Veterans being honored, chaplains connecting with families regarding essential medications, supplies and skilled nurses available around the clock. We've also known many cases where individuals "graduate" from Hospice and begin to get healthier and stronger with a team of professionals on hand.

Being careful not to skip around too much or make too many moves too quickly will prevent what we call transition trauma. Think about how long your mom or dad have been in one place and ask yourself if moving would be more of a health hazard or less. Consider our natural ability to use cognitive mapping when eye sight and dementia are in the picture, when anything is moved around it can cause emotional issues like anger, depression and confusion. If the move is the right decision then always give it at least a month to allow for this transition time to pass and for hope and new friendships to rise.

All in all, I want to leave you with a mission. Whether you are an hour away, 3,000 miles away or living next door your parent(s) need you. They may have been the best or they may have been crummy, but they are going into a time of needing you to be strong. The hardest things to do in life are things that demand our self-sacrifice and servant heart, but they are the most life giving.

I tell families all the time that the best care a family can provide is for a loving family member to be there every step of the way. Begin with answering the big questions and surrounding yourself with a qualified and loving team, continue the communication with synchronized and systemized plans that give you peace of mind. Last of all never miss out on the beauty of need.

The bond of parents caring for their children and children caring for their parents is one of the most beautiful and natural gifts that you can receive. Not everyone gets this gift. Cherish time with your family young and old, listen to all the wonderful and funny stories, use your strengths to lift each other up. Even if you can't always hold them in your arms you will hold them in your heart.

[1] Pierret, Charles. (2006) The 'sandwich generation': women caring for parents and children

Chapter 25- Alone- The Parent Left Behind
Page Cole

53 years… that's how long Ted & Martha had been married. They met in their junior year of high school, fell in love and the rest, as they say, was history. They'd spent a wonderful lifetime together- three children, seven grandchildren, five different cities spanning three different career tracks. Their golden years of retirement had been prepared for well. Finances were not a challenge and at 67 years of age, they began that next exciting phase of their journey together. Life had been good to them both and it was only getting better!

Fast forward to their 53rd year of marriage. Ted and Martha had been enjoying retirement, traveling and grandkids for the last six years and loving every minute of it. Then, Ted began to notice a discomfort in his abdomen and soon the pain began to intensify. Following a visit to the doctor and a battery of tests, the news came back and it wasn't good. It was cancer and it was in advanced stages. No treatments or surgeries could stop the inevitable. The doctor shared the somber news that they could count on three months, maybe six months at the most to prepare for the end.

Four months to the day following Ted's diagnosis his family gathered around his graveside. Now what? Ted was the foundation of this family, the rock everyone depended on. Although no one said it out loud, the same thought was running through all of their minds… "What do we do now?"

Grieving is a process

All families will encounter grief at some point on their life journey. Dying is as much a part of life as living is. Understand that everyone in the family deals with grief in their own way and in their own time. The Kubler-Ross model of the Seven Stages of Grief reminds us that most, if not all, will pass through the following stages of dealing with their own grief:

1. **Shock-** initial paralysis at hearing the bad news;
2. **Denial-** trying to avoid the inevitable;
3. **Anger-** frustrated outpouring of bottled up emotion;
4. **Bargaining-** Seeking in vain for a way out;
5. **Depression-** Final realization of the inevitable;

6. **Testing-** Seeking realistic solutions;
7. **Acceptance-** Finally finding a way forward.

As you help a surviving parent work through their own journey of grief, it is important that you understand, accept and affirm for their sake and yours that this is not a decision, it is not something they have to "move on" past, but a process they will most likely be working through and dealing with on a daily basis for the rest of their life. There is not only one right way, time frame or manner that is the best or most healthy way to work through grief. Where a spouse went through any kind of illness before dying, the remaining spouse will have already begun the grieving process.

Caring for their physical needs

One of the challenges the surviving parent will most likely face is making sure that their own physical needs are adequately cared for. Loss of appetite, diminished physical activity and the toll that increased stress and/or depression can take on their physical body can be damaging, even dangerous.

Some individuals may need assistance in this area with very simple tasks, like shopping for groceries, cooking meals or even preparing their plate and taking it to them. Hydration is incredibly important as well and if you sense they are not drinking enough liquids, it might be necessary to chart their liquid intake to insure they are drinking enough water to stay healthy. The health of a surviving spouse is at great risk following the death of their mate and working to make sure they are eating healthy and drinking enough fluids is one way to diminish the chances of their health being jeopardized.

It is important that members of the family are consistent in monitoring their parents' food and liquid intake to insure they are not making their own physical condition worse. You might consider suggesting to them that they add Boost or Ensure nutritional drinks to their daily dietary regiment. These are packed with vital nutrients to help their baseline intake steady and the bare minimum intake of their daily nutrients consistent.

Be patient with them as they express their grief:

Although the Seven Stages of Grief are fairly consistent among all people dealing with the loss of a loved one, the ways they work through those phases and express themselves through those stages vary greatly. One person may want to share memories and talk incessantly about the loved one who died. Others may go into a dark funk or depression and not want to talk at all.

Expressions of anger or despair are common and even spoken desires of wanting to die and join their spouse are not abnormal expressions. They are not, and it is not... I repeat, it is NOT your job to fix them, correct them or scold them. It is not your responsibility to pull them out of their depression or encourage them to be "realistic". Your job is simple: be there, be patient, and love them.

Listen:

This may be one of the most important things you can do for the surviving parent. The natural tendency for children who have hurting parents is to try and "fix" the situation. That might include planning things to keep them busy, talking about anything BUT the parent who died or using whatever means necessary to distract them from their grief. This tendency, although natural and instinctive, does more harm than good. Instead, choose the hard thing: listen. It may mean working through hurtful emotions if the illness that lead to the death was long and drawn out. On the other hand, listening may involve longer, more uncomfortable periods of sitting in silence together.

The story goes that one day Elizabeth Johnson passed away, leaving her elderly husband Curtis alone. They lived in an average suburban neighborhood, surrounded by families and homes with their busy lives and hectic schedules. The Thompson family was their next door neighbor and the youngest Thompson child was a five-year old girl named Susie. She loved the Johnsons and had spent a lot of time at their home in the past. She made cookies with Elizabeth and Curtis let her watch him in his woodshop as he built things for family and friends. A few days after Elizabeth's funeral, Suzie came in the front door of their house with a smile on her face and tears in her eyes. Her mother was worried something terrible had happened, but was confused by the sad little smile on Susie's face. "Why are you crying?", she asked. "I went next door to see Mr. Johnson and he was sitting on his front porch alone. He was crying," she said to her mother. "I didn't know what to say, so I just sat down next to him, and I cried with him."

Sometimes the wisdom of children is amazing. Listen. Be still. Hug them if they need it. Cry with them when you can. Be there for them, and be available for their heartache to have a place to land.

Acknowledge important dates and anniversaries

Finally, understand that the first year following any death of a loved one is typically the hardest time. There will be a myriad of "first" dates where they will need special compassion, understanding and presence from those who love them. Those "first" dates include all of those special holidays, personal or family events or anniversaries that the surviving parent used to be able to celebrate with their sweetheart, but now have to spend alone. Those would include the first Christmas, Thanksgiving, Valentine's Day, wedding anniversary and both of their birthdays. In addition, events like grandchildren being born, or graduating or getting married can also be events that bring a certain level or melancholy or sadness to them. Talk about those upcoming dates with other family members and make sure everyone is sensitive to the emotional challenge those events might bring to the senior who has lost a mate.

Life happens. Death is a part of it. You can help them with both.

Chapter 26- Keeping the Brain Young

Tina Moore

What do you consider the most important aspects of good heath? A good diet? Definitely! Some sort of physical exercise? Absolutely! However, we often overlook two very important elements: mind stimulation and brain exercise.

When we are young, school does its part to keep both of these things in check. As we get a little older, our jobs, families and activities keep our cognitive functions advancing. But, as we begin to reach retirement age, we slow down. The slower pace usually means less personal contact and communication with people. No longer working in a job means fewer decisions and thought processes throughout the day. While we certainly deserve the break at retirement, we must be aware that our mind and brain needs activity to stay healthy.

Cognitive Training

In 2006, scientists completed a study of cognitive training in older adults. This study, Advanced Cognitive Training for Independent and Vital Elderly

(ACTIVE), was the first of its kind to demonstrate the positive effects of cognitive or mental training in older adults.

In January 2014, an updated report on this study appeared in the Journal of the American Geriatrics Society. This report extended the validity of brain training ten years after the start of the study, meaning that brain training was still paying off after ten years! Wow! The findings showed training gains for aspects of cognition involved in the ability to think and learn. The report indicated, "Longer term results indicate that particular types of cognitive training can provide a lasting benefit a decade later. They suggest that we should continue to pursue cognitive training as an intervention that might help maintain the mental abilities of older people so that they may remain independent and in the community," said NIA Director Richard J. Hodes, M.D.

In short, the good news is that cognitive training could help seniors remain independent. The not so good news is many seniors live alone and cognitive training is absent in their lives and difficult to achieve. Back to some good news... I have some tips and information on simple and easy methods to improve cognitive skills and also help to slow down the loss of mental abilities.

Case Study: Sharon

First, I would like to share an inspiring story to illustrate the benefits of companionship of family, friends and caregivers; participation in a variety of activities; and having fun in the moment.

Marce is one of the most vibrant and compassionate caregivers you could ever encounter. She has brought much life and love to all of her care recipients, especially Sharon.

Sharon is a retired legal secretary. She is widowed with no children, but has a vast extended family who graciously tend to all her needs. When Sharon could no longer live independently and safe at home, she moved into an assisted living facility. From day one, she repeatedly asked to go back home. She was very unhappy and depressed. Sharon, who is only

72, is in great physical condition, but suffers from dementia. Her family personally selected Marce to visit Sharon twice a week in hopes of lifting her spirit. They were fast friends and are much more like sisters than a caregiver and her client. The best measure of success is that Sharon no longer asks to go home; she now looks forward to her time with Marce.

Here are a few ways Marce identified Sharon's interests and put them into plans for activities:

1) Marce quickly noticed that Sharon still has strong connections and interests with secretarial work. She provided Sharon with an adding machine, the kind that printed the calculations on paper. Marce saves her store receipts, gives them to Sharon and tells her the front desk needs the total. This results in Sharon working her brain functions. It also makes her feel worthy and important.

2) Marce took Sharon's secretarial interests a step further when she received permission from the assisted living facility to use a spare closet to setup a small office setting for Sharon. She provided the office with supplies, file folders, papers and a donated electric typewriter. Soon the office became such a great idea that the facility decided to relocate it to the common area for all the residents to enjoy.

3) Sharon is very mobile and in great physical shape. This allows Marce to venture into activities of a physical nature. Free-throw contests at the gym, hitting golf balls at the driving range, riding go-karts and walks in the park are just a few of the activities Sharon and Marce enjoy.

4) Sometimes the simple ideas are the best. Marce keeps a variety of hats on hand for all her clients to enjoy. From floppy sun hats to baseball caps, the hats provide clients with the option of how they want to look and feel that day.

While Marce is our caregiver, her clients know her best as a friend, singing companion, picnic planner, dance partner, sports coach and, of course, explorer of their next adventure!

> *"Creating a new road map for cognitive health provides a new window of opportunity to promote health equity."*
>
> *J. Neil Henderson, PhD, University of Oklahoma*

Mind Stimulation- Lifestyle Changes for Mind Stimulation

The current generation of senior citizens grew up and raised families in an era where there was considerable routine in many households. For example: laundry on Monday, ironing on Tuesday and so on. Even specific meals were scheduled on certain days of the week. Life was certainly more precise and predictable back in their day. Many seniors continue to live in those traditions. While those routines remain safe to some seniors, they could also be limiting the stimulation of their minds. At this point, the familiar actions ultimately put the brain on cruise control. Little thought is needed to process those actions that have been repeated thousands of times throughout the years.

How can you spark mind stimulation for your loved ones stuck in their routines? You certainly do not want to upset the proverbial apple cart. After all, things have been running smoothly for so many years. Instead, find innovative ways to slightly alter their schedule. Attitude, tone and general communication is crucial. Similar to dealing with a child, it is important to pick your battles. When trying to improve their well-being with something that is basically optional, be sure to use methods of suggestion and encouragement. They may resent and sometimes refuse notions given as demands. It may take some creative thinking on your part, but clever proposals can go a long way in terms of succeeding with change. As an example, you may mention to your loved one that by doing laundry on Fridays all the clothes would be clean for the weekend. It sounds basic, but even little tweaks, such as changing tasks to different days, will inspire the mind to analyze how the change could impact the entire week. Even if they ponder the idea for a few minutes or think on it for a few days, you've accomplished your primary goal of mind stimulation.

Conversations for Mind Stimulation

Another idea to encourage mind stimulation takes just a bit of planning on the part of loved ones and caregivers. Always be thinking of future communications you will have with your loved ones. Jot down notes throughout the day. Plan your questions and topics to begin dialogs and not just simple responses. Perhaps begin planning with a list of cognitive elements you want to reach and devise questions that will utilize those elements. What kinds of questions are most beneficial? Always ask questions that will spur thought and discussion. Avoid questions they could answer with one or two words.

Creative Cognitive Communications

Memory: What did you make for dinner last night and how did you prepare it? What model and year was the first brand new car you purchased? Do you remember the names of our neighbors when I was a kid?

Reasoning: What do you think about planting more perennial flowers instead of annual flowers?

Confidence: How do you make your gravy so smooth? Could you tell me your secret?

Concentration: What time do you think we should leave for the doctor's appointment if we stop by the bank on the way?

Activities for Mind Stimulation

Activities can be incredibly mind stimulating for seniors. In particular, those activities that achieve learning, encourage interaction with others, create smiles and laughter, promote confidence, or essentially any activity that draws out feelings or emotions that would otherwise be absent.

Are there volunteer opportunities suitable for your loved one? Check within the community, local senior centers, churches and non-profit organizations for ideas. This is a wonderful way to accomplish mind stimulation on many levels. This gratifying mission could be a great way to encourage communication with others and allow the use of their minds and hands to help. It also does wonders for their confidence. The heartwarming results of volunteering are limitless!

Consider activities that link to their former jobs or hobbies. Did they work on the railroad or collect model trains? They could visit a transportation or train museum. Perhaps they would enjoy a short trip on Amtrak.

Is there an interest or hobby that got their attention later in life? A hobby they loved, but never took the time to pursue? Check out the local craft stores to see if any classes would be of interest and suitable for your loved one. Go online to see what local senior centers offer. Sometimes community or senior centers offer computer classes and have various groups for things like quilting or playing cards. If they have a hobby that is not supported anywhere, mention it to the senior center to see if they could initiate a group or maybe they know of other seniors who may be interested in getting together to support the hobby or interest.

Have fun! Pack a picnic lunch and go to the park. Stroll around the park and identify various plants and animals. Inquire about the smells they can recognize. Play "I Spy" and provide prompts and help, as needed.

Think outside the box! Brainstorm to identify activities that your loved one has never done. Have they been to an arcade? Have they ever been to a go-kart track? Hit golf balls at the driving range? Fed ducks at the park? Have they browsed the Internet, perhaps to look at pictures of their favorite actor or favorite flower? Have they talked to someone using electronic, face-to-face technology, such as FaceTime on Apple devices? There are infinite possibilities for activities that will help exercise their brain.

Benefits of an Active Lifestyle
The National Institute on Aging says that research of older people with an active lifestyle could have the following benefits:

> - **Are less likely to develop certain disease.** Participating in hobbies and other social and leisure pursuits may lower risk for developing health problems including dementia.
> - **Have a longer lifespan.** One study showed that older adults who reported taking part in social activities (such as playing games, belonging to social groups, or traveling) or meaningful, productive activities (such as having a paid or unpaid job, or gardening) lived longer than people who did not. Researchers are further exploring this connection.
> - **Are happier and less depressed.** Studies suggest that older adults who participate in what they believe are meaningful activities like volunteering in their communities, say they feel happier and healthier. One study placed older adults from an urban community in their neighborhood public elementary schools to tutor children 15 hours a week. Volunteers reported personal satisfaction from the experience. The researchers found it improved the volunteers' cognitive and physical health, as well as the children's school success. They think it might also have long-term benefits, lowering the older adults' risk of

developing disability, dependency, and dementia in later life.

➢ **Are better prepared to cope with loss.** Studies suggest that volunteering can help with stress and depression from the death of a spouse. Among people who experienced a loss, those who took part in volunteer activities felt more positive about their own abilities (reported greater self-efficacy).

➢ **May be able to improve their thinking abilities.** Another line of research is exploring how participating in creative arts might help people age well. For example, recent studies have shown that older adults' memory, creativity, comprehension, and problem-solving abilities improved after an intensive, 4-week (8-session) acting course. Other studies are providing new information about ways that creative activities like music or dance can help older adults.

These are just a few of the benefits noted from various research studies. The improvements you notice in your loved ones may vary depending on factors of their deficiencies.

Brain Exercise- Understanding Functions in the Brain

Brain exercise takes mind stimulation a step further. Cognitive brain exercise focuses on each specific area of the brain and their roles. To better explain, we will step through each major region of the brain and describe some of functions that relate to each general section. The level of ability or deficiency of specific brain functions will vary for each person. The levels may also vary depending on the day, time or specific moment of the analysis.

We begin with the **frontal lobe** portion of the brain that controls "executive functions" such as judgement, emotional response and personality. When this area is declining, it may cause impairments in behavior, personality, emotions, organization, attention, concentration and language. Selecting activities and prompting conversations that will initiate problem solving, planning, concentration and general speaking is helpful to exercise this area of the brain.

The **parietal lobe** involves information processed through visual perception, sense of touch and the differentiation of size, shape and color. Some of the language and reading functions are also involved. If deficiencies exist with these functions, activities to heighten sight and touch will help to engage this area of the brain. Identifying items only by touch is a very good way to encourage brain activity in the parietal lobe.

The **temporal lobe** involves the functions of memory, hearing, musical awareness and understanding language. A good way to bring together the functions of hearing, music and memory is to play familiar songs from various eras of their life. Another exercise is to play a game thinking of synonyms for words or pick category and a letter of the alphabet and see how many things you can name, such as fruits/vegetables beginning with the letter "P".

The area of the **occipital lobe** involves vision, reading and processing visual information. Any type of reading or visual game is helpful to benefit this area of the brain.

The **cerebellum** involves more of the physical aspects of coordination of voluntary movements, balance, posture and equilibrium. Playing catch with a small, lightweight ball is an excellent activity for physical exercise and brain training in the cerebellum.

The **brain stem** helps control breathing, swallowing, heart rate, digestion, balance and ability to sleep.

START TODAY

Mind stimulation and brain exercise is critical at any age. In our younger years we naturally get more exposure to events that stimulate our brain. However, as we grow older and our lives begin to slow down, so does our connection to activities that keep our brain young. Seniors should consciously do something each day that will not only exercise their body, but also stimulate and exercise the brain. It doesn't have to be life altering. It doesn't even need to cost a lot of money; it just needs to be energizing for the brain.

What should you do first? R.O.S. Therapy Systems has created a simple structure to initiate activities into the lives of seniors. The Four Pillars of Activities are shown below. [R.O.S. Therapy Systems, LLC, Activities for the Family Caregiver – Dementia – How to Engage, How to Live by Scott Silknitter, Robert D. Brennan, RN, NHA, MS, CDP and Dawn Worsley, ADC/MC/EDU, CDP]

1st Pillar of Activities – Know your Loved One – Information Gathering and Assessment – Have a Personal History Form completed. Know them – who they are, who they were and what their functional abilities are today. Make sure all caregivers know this as well. You can find the Personal History Form and links to free activity apps at www.StartSomeJoy.com, a website from the founder of R.O.S Therapy Systems.

2nd Pillar of Activities – Communicating and Motivating for Success – Communication is key. Each caregiver must know how to effectively communicate with your loved one and be consistent with techniques.

3rd Pillar of Activities – Customary Routines and Preferences – As best as possible, maintain a routine and daily plan based on your loved one's needs and preferences.

4th Pillar of Activities – Planning and Executing Activities – Based on all the information you have gathered about your loved one, you have the opportunity to offer engaging activities that are appropriate and meet your loved one's personal preferences.

With the Four Pillars of Activities completed, or at least in mind, here are a few basic ideas to encourage brain activity on a daily basis. Depending on the individual, you may want to begin slowly with just one method or perhaps describe a few and let them choose.

> - **READ** - Reading of any type will help influence brain activity. If your loved one doesn't enjoy chapter books, perhaps try an inspirational book with daily readings or subscribe them to a magazine that highlights a hobby or interest.
> - **WRITE** – Maintain lists for needed groceries and plans for upcoming meals. Purchase a notebook and encourage writing notes as a daily journal. On the inside, front cover, include a short list of ideas of what to include in the journal. Some examples may include: what they ate that day; who they talked with or saw during the day; important news events; something they learned; activities and exercises completed; and things accomplished.
> - **GAMES** – Puzzles, such as crossword, seek and find and traditional jigsaw puzzles, are easy sources of brain stimulation, especially for seniors who live alone. It is great when two or more can play games such as cards, dominos and board games.
> - **COMMUNICATION** – Communication is a vital part of life. Be sure your loved one, especially those who live alone, receives as much verbal communication as possible. If necessary, set a schedule with family

members for at least one person to call each day of the week.

> **ACTIVITIES** – Any activity, new or familiar, will provide brain stimulation. Use information from the Personal History Form to help develop ideas for a variety of activities.

Find the Right Balance

Everyone has different limits to the amount of time they can spend on social or other activities. What is perfect for one person might be too much for another. Be careful not to take on too much at once. You might start by adding one or two activities to your routine and see how you feel. You can always add more. Remember—participating in activities you enjoy should be fun, not stressful.

National Institute on Aging Information Center, April 2015, NIH Publication No. 15-7411

At Visiting Angels, our goal is to keep your loved ones safe at home for as long as possible. We help maintain their independence of daily routines and enhance their quality of life. We know from personal and professional experience that activities to stimulate the mind and exercise the brain can be incredibly beneficial to the overall health of seniors. I truly hope you find this information enlightening and that it challenges you to seek creative ways to keep the brain young!

Author Bios

Dominique Alvarez

Dominique is the co-owner of the Chino and Diamond Bar Visiting Angels offices in Southern California, serving their communities for almost 10 years. She has always worked hands on with people whether it was volunteering in local city politics, the Special Olympics, or as PTA President; this extended to her professional life at Xerox and working as an Instructional Aide in an Autism focused pre-school.

Dominique still lives in the community where she grew up and is a single mother of two teenagers, one with special needs. Through life experiences with her son and aging parents it has given her the unique perspective of identifying with the struggles her families face and helping them navigate those with the help of exceptional care.
Email: chinoangels@gmail.com   Twitter: @Chinoangels,
LinkedIn: www.linkedin.com/in/dominique-alvarez-21b547a3

William Bruck

William joined the United States Army in 1992, and has served four tours of duty overseas, as well as completing Military Intelligence School. William graduated from Northland Baptist Bible College, graduated from ALBAT as a journeyman linesman, graduated from Warrant Officer Candidate school, and received his MBA in Project Management from Southern Columbia University.

He currently holds the rank of CW3 in the Wisconsin National Guard. He owns a Visiting Angels franchise in Monroe, Michigan, and has received numerous local and national awards for his personal service, professional activities and work with his Visiting Angels franchise. He is also the recipient of a number of medals for his military service, including two bronze stars. He is married to his wife Natalie and is the proud father of 7 children.
Email: wbruck@visitingangels.com

Page Cole

Page has been developing leaders for over 30 years as a pastor with his last role as Executive Pastor of First Baptist Church, Owasso. He currently owns Visiting Angels of Green Country, a non-medical home health company, with offices in Tulsa, Owasso and Bartlesville, Oklahoma. His passion continues to be in mentoring young leaders. He's husband to Ronda, and dad to Erin, Nathan & Ben. He has authored several books, including *"Protecting Your Nest Egg: Fraud Protection for Senior Citizens from Con Artists, Thieves & Scams"*. He also created the free iTunes app & companion book *LifeChest*, designed to help people manage the care needs for their aging parents. He serves actively in First Baptist Church of Owasso, OK, and has served as president of the Oklahoma Partnership for Home Care.
Facebook: www.facebook.com/VisitingAngelsTulsaMetro
Twitter: @pagecole
LinkedIn: www.linkedin.com/in/pagecole
Website: www.visitingangels.com/tulsa.

Debra Desrosiers

Debra is the Director of Visiting Angels in Auburn, New Hampshire and joined the Visiting Angels franchise in 2004. Debra is a Certified Senior Advisor, Certified Alzheimer's/Dementia Coach/Consultant and Home Care Certification with a specialization in Memory Care. Prior to joining the Visiting Angels family Debra was employed as a corporate controller in the car rental industry managing multiple locations. In 2014 Debra established another company called Caregiver Keys to help both families and professionals with specialized education, coaching and consulting specifically in dementia care. Debra has also given many seminars in the local area to help educate the local communities.

Debra grew up in Manchester, NH, went to high school at Memorial High School in Manchester NH, and college at Southern New Hampshire

University and recently obtained her Coaching Certificate from the University of New Hampshire. Debra now resides in Auburn, NH with her husband Ron and son Jesse whom also work in the family business, and another son, Alex, and three dogs. In Debra's spare time she enjoys providing Pet Therapy with her Golden Retriever, Sonny, and volunteers with Alzheimer's Association MA/NH chapter.

Email: visitingangelsnh@comcast.net

Website: www.visitingangels.com/auburn www.caregiverkeys.com,

Facebook: www.facebook.com/VisitingAngelsAuburnNH,

LinkedIn: www.linkedin.com/in/debradesrosiers

David Forman

For more than 30 years, David has owned and operated a successful public relations and marketing firm. His company FCW, Inc serves local and well-known national and international clients from a wide variety of industries, including consumer products, wine and spirits, fashion, beauty, electronics, home furnishings, business-to-business and non-profit. He is widely recognized as a media expert, Fortune 500 consultant and newspaper columnist. He is the author of *Publicity Professor*, a resource that teaches individuals, organization and businesses how to generate publicity. David and his wife Annalise moved from the NYC area to start their Visiting Angels franchise in Southern Delaware in 2013. Information about his company and book can be found at delawarepublicity.com.

Website: http://publicityprofessorbook.com

Website: http://delawarepublicity.com/Home.html

Email: Dforman@visitingangels.com

Paul Gach

Paul is the co-owner of Visiting Angels of Charlotte, NC. He has been serving families of Charlotte Metro and Concord areas for 13 years. His experience has been both personal and professional, which has proven that home care maintains people's feelings of self-worth and benefits entire families. His passion for providing quality care and educating families has earned Visiting Angels of Charlotte the Provider of Choice award from Home Care Pulse numerous times. Sharing information about taking away the keys is a topic Paul has experience with his own family. Between his parents and in-laws he has had to deal with the easiest response of taking away the keys, being "That's fine I do not want to drive.", to the very emotional response of great loss and depression, to the hardest requiring involving medical professionals and the Department of Motor Vehicles. Paul brings a wealth of expertise and personal experience to this very difficult topic.
Email: PaulGach@visitingangels.com
Facebook: www.facebook.com/VisitingAngelsCharlotteNC
Website: www.visitingangels.com/charlotte

Debbie Harrison

Debbie was born in Toronto, Canada to an immigrant Irish father and the daughter of Scottish immigrants. Her parents and siblings immigrated to the US when she was a toddler where they settled into Pico Rivera, California (a suburb of East L.A.). In 1980 she moved to Alaska where she married and raised a family. She had a diverse career in hospitality, direct sales, Church and Real Estate. Debbie, her husband and their children have always enjoyed the company of seniors and advocated on their behalf. Debbie is the co-owner of Visiting Angels of Grand Junction Colorado.
Email: DHarrison@VisitingAngels.com
Website: www.visitingangels.com/GrandJunction
Facebook: www.facebook.com/VisitingAngelsGrandJunction

Valerie Hentzschel

Valerie is the owner/director of Visiting Angels in Prescott, Arizona. Her background is in social work. She earned her MSW in 2006 from Cal State San Bernardino. Valerie served as a social worker in various older adult programs in San Bernardino County for 15 years where she worked together with Visiting Angels on multiple occasions which led her to purchase her own franchise in 2014. Valerie and her husband Gary now make Prescott their home.

Email: vhentzschel@visitingangels.com
Website: www.visitingangels.com/prescott

Patty Laychock

Patty is the co-owner of Visiting Angels of Atlantic County, New Jersey. She and her sister bring over 20 years of experience in healthcare; Kathy is an RN, and Patty is a Respiratory Therapist. They both have experience in all areas of patient care, including critical care, post op care, rehabilitation, sub-acute, long term care and home care. Since opening their Visiting Angels franchise in 2005, they have both become Certified Dementia Practitioners. Patty has also earned her Certified Senior Advisor as well.

Email: VisitingSisters@comcast.net

Gail Lohman

In business seven years with her husband, Bill, Gail's experience in the field comes from a life-long love of serving seniors as well as spending more than 15 years working for state-wide nursing home associations. Having spent many years volunteering with seniors choosing in-home care as a business was personal. Gail have a vested interest in caring for seniors and it fits well with her personal beliefs and is exactly where she wants to be — helping people stay in their homes. It is a service and a calling. A business that supports her family and makes her feel good about what she does while creating jobs for others. Gail is the co-owner of Visiting Angels of Eldorado in Cameron Park, California.

Facebook: www.facebook.com/VisitingAngelsElDorado

Website: www.visitingangels.com/eldorado

Margaret Maczulski

Margaret is the owner and managing director of Visiting Angels Libertyville, Illinois, a home care agency licensed by the State of Illinois and associated with over 550 Visiting Angels businesses in North America. She has held this position for over eight years in the northern suburbs of Chicago developing quality caregiving to serve the elder population in the community. Margaret is a Detroit native, having graduated from Michigan State University with a Bachelor of Science degree in Retailing and Business Administration. After a successful career with a Fortune consumer products company, she took a new path. Her experiences growing up in a medical family and her familiarities with home care needs with her own mother made her decide to help seniors stay safely and comfortably in their own homes with Visiting Angels.

Margaret is active in Lake County senior services, belonging to several groups which service this population. She holds certifications from the University of Southern California, Davis School of Gerontology and the National Certification Council for Activity Professionals and has studied the CSA program. Her strongest desire is to help those in need stay as independent and active as possible. In doing so, they will be healthier and content.

Email: maczulski@visitingangels.com

Website: www.VisitingAngels.com/Libertyville

Facebook: www.facebook.com/VisitingAngelsLibertyville

Bob Melcher

Bob spent 26 years in the corporate world as a Brand Manager and marketing executive before starting a Visiting Angels franchise. He works helping seniors live in comfort and safety in Fairfield, Connecticut as an owner/operator of the Visiting Angels franchise he owns. Website: www.visitingangels.com/fairfield

David Milby

David is a very active owner with Visiting Angels. For 8 years he and his team have been providing Home Care Excellence in the Middle Georgia area. He still makes time to meet with each and every family, leading discussions on safety, care plans, family dynamics and connections with the community. He has been a guest speaker and educator at many local meetings and events and loves to make that personal connection with everyone he meets.

David and his brother William started Visiting Angels of Central GA in 2008 with their father Bill Milby. David lives in Kathleen, GA with his wife Sandra and 3 girls (Abby, Reagan and Adele) who are also active with the company (they get to do all the fun stuff). He is grateful and thankful to his full team of administration and nursing staff for the growth and success of Visiting Angels Home Care of Central GA.
Facebook: www.facebook.com/VisitingAngelsMacon
Website: www.visitingangels.com/centralga

Tina Moore

Tina is the proud owner of Visiting Angels in Belleville, Illinois. Her agency has been in business for over 10 years providing exceptional in-home care with respect and compassion. The agency's goal to support and enhance the quality of life for care recipients while

allowing them to continue living in their familiar surroundings has been fulfilled hundreds of times throughout the years.

Tina attended St. Louis University and worked for MetLife for 24 years before opening Visiting Angels in 2006. She currently serves as a member of the Home Health Advisory Committee for the Illinois Department of Public Health. Tina and Rob, her husband of 25 years, along with their two sons, Connor and Lucas, reside in Waterloo, Illinois.
Website: www.VisitingAngels.com/Belleville
Facebook: www.facebook.com/VisitingAngelsBellevilleIllinois
Email: TMoore@VisitingAngels.com

Eddie Morris

Eddie is sympathetic to the often stressful situations occurring with convalescent care, chronic illnesses, dementia related issues and the end of life process of a loved one. She was raised by her grandparents and learned from an early age, the cycle of struggles that people face as their bodies grow weaker while their minds fight for independence. She serves her community so that she can improve the quality of life for seniors, their families and their providers. Eddie is the current owner/director of Visiting Angels Ponca City, OK.
Email: emorris@visitingangels.com
Website: www.visitingangels.com/poncacity
Facebook: www.facebook.com/VisitingAngelsofPoncaCity
Twitter: https://twitter.com/VisitingAngelPC

Susie Murray

Susie is a graduate of Kennesaw State University with over 20 years of business experience in banking, finance, and mortgage lending. In 2013 she opened a Visiting Angels franchise in Cleveland, GA with her husband, Kevin. During their twenty-year marriage

Susie and Kevin have lived on both coasts, as well as in Japan and in Germany, while Kevin served in the United States Army.

After Kevin's retirement, they looked for a way to fulfill their dream of owning their own business and were drawn to the home care market due to their experience with the aging and end of life care needs of their own family members. Kevin continued to deploy to Afghanistan as a civilian intelligence expert until 2016, and is now a full time college student and splitting child rearing duties of their seven-year-old son. Susie is continuing to grow and expand their business, and trying to keep a lid on all of the shenanigans.
Email: smurray@visitingangels.com
Facebook: www.facebook.com/Visiting-Angels-of-Northeast-Georgia-493085114083429/
Website: www.visitingangels.com/northeastgeorgia

Deborah Waldecker

Deborah has been a Visiting Angels agency owner since 2004-- operating out of Sun City Center, Florida. She is a Certified Senior Advisor and her agency is certified by the National Certification Council for Activity Professionals. The office is often times visited by her little dog, Zeus, who provides endless entertainment, compassion and joy to whoever he encounters.

Deborah has a Bachelor's Degree in Healthcare Administration and has attended school at Rutgers University, Valencia Community College, and Florida Hospital College of the Health Sciences. Deborah also graduated from ECPI University in Virginia Beach, Virginia with a degree in Medical Records Technology. Deborah holds a Life, Health and Variable Annuity License which helps her to assist her clients with all of their health insurance and long term care plan questions.

Her background first began in the 80's where she worked at Eastern Virginia Medical School and then Humana Hospital. She relocated to

Florida from Virginia to work for Humana Hospital, and then began working with physicians doing contracting/network development and concurrent review for a few large Medicare HMO's. Deborah left her last position of 5 years at Wellcare of Florida where she served as Director of Provider Relations to start her own Visiting Angels agency.

Website: www.visitingangels.com/Hillsborough

Facebook: www.facebook.com/visitingangelssuncitycenter

_____

Made in the USA
Middletown, DE
11 September 2016